REBIRTH

REBIRTH

The Tibetan Game of Liberation

Mark Tatz and Jody Kent

RIDER & COMPANY

Rider & Company
3 Fitzroy Square, London W1P 6JD

An imprint of the Hutchinson Publishing Group

London Melbourne Sydney Auckland
Wellington Johannesburg and agencies
throughout the world

First published in Great Britain 1978

Printed in Great Britain by The Anchor Press Ltd
and bound by Wm Brendon & Son Ltd
both of Tiptree, Essex

ISBN 0 09 136051 X

To the Dezhung Rinpoche, learned and accomplished, who has given his gracious blessing to the publication of this game ("It will bring great benefit"), to Lama Trinlay Drubpa and others who have favored it with advice and helped in its presentation, and of course to the understanding Lady of Enlightenment.

May any merit deriving from this work be dedicated to the welfare of all living beings.

CONTENTS

ILLUSTRATIONS

Preface

The Game of Rebirth reveals the Tibetan Buddhist map of the universe. The scroll painting or "board" lays out a cosmic geography, presenting one's possibilities of future rebirth, and demonstrates the paths to liberation and the forms of enlightenment. In the course of playing this game the players' tendencies toward certain destinations are revealed, and guidelines are presented for their transcendence of ordinary existence and attainment of future states that are free from suffering.

Rebirth was invented in the early part of the thirteenth century by Sakya pandita Kunga Gyaltsen ("Whose Banner Is Total Joy"), the great Sanskrit scholar of the Sakya sect. He created it to amuse his ailing mother, for it was considered unhealthy—even for the sick—to sleep during the day.

Later, Tibetans regarded it as an educational game, inculcating in children the Buddhist map of the world and an understanding of the workings of karma. It was also enjoyed as an amusement, and played by young and old, lay and monastic, with great merriment and jesting at the karmic tendencies that are revealed by the cast of the die. Tibetans were very fond of games of dice, and often there was betting on the outcome. In monasteries it was enjoyed on holidays by the elders, and by the young during long afternoons following rituals and study. Mr. Thubten Norbu, elder brother of the present Dalai Lama, describes how it was played during his childhood at school:

> The winner was rewarded with a prize of sweets. Sometimes such a game would last for hours, and occasionally it would

get very noisy. Particularly fortunate or unfortunate throws were greeted with a chorus of congratulations or groans as the case might be.*

Laypeople were especially fond of playing the game during the summer picnic and camping holidays by the rivers. It is still enjoyed in the Tibetan-culture areas of Sikkim and Bhutan and by refugees in various parts of the world. Tibetans who have not seen the game since exile greet its sight or mention with a laugh and a smile, as though at the memory of happier days.

The present version, with 104 squares, was painted by Pema Dorje, a young layman of a Nyingma family living in India. The original of Sakya pandita and other modern versions are also reproduced for purposes of comparison. The game is provided with an introduction covering its background, philosophic premises, and layout; a set of instructions on how to play; and individual commentaries of each square on the states of rebirth and stages of the paths to happiness.

Each player begins in the "human realm," moving in accord with the cast of a die. Depending on one's karma, one proceeds upward or downward on the board into higher or lower states of rebirth, mapping out the potential destinations of one's future lives. The main classes of living beings in the world and the various regions and philosophies of humanity are in the lower rows. One may be reborn among the classes of gods or demons, ghosts or animals, or in one of the hells. The object of the game is to enter one of the paths to enlightenment and follow it successfully to the top. On the way are magic lands, high meditative states, and tantric attainments. The winner is the first to reach Buddhahood and enter nirvana.

---

* Thubten Norbu, *Tibet Is My Country,* as told to Heinrich Harrer, trans. Edward Fitzgerald, (London: Hart-Davis, 1960), p. 93

·°❧ *Introduction* ❧°·

☞ I ☜

BUDDHISM IN TIBET

The various elements of Tibetan cultural life came from widely divergent sources. Situated in the heart of Asia, it received cultural influence from all sides. Yet from their lofty perch in the Himalayas the Tibetans were generally free to choose what they wished to retain. From the fourteenth century on the country was threatened and dominated by the Mongolians and Manchurians, and finally overcome by Chinese military might. Among the aristocracy, who usually dealt with the invaders, modifications of language, food, and dress were sustained under East Asian influence. But above all, in ancient and medieval times the Tibetans chose to adopt the Buddhist traditions of northern India. Their culture was strikingly defined by this choice, historically curious because it was so intentional and because it necessitated overcoming such formidable geographic barriers as the dense jungles of India and the high Himalayas. Until 1951, when the Chinese marched into Lhasa Tibet remained the secret remnant of a medieval spirituality that was spread at one time over most of the civilized world.[1]

In the seventh and eighth centuries A.D. the religion of the majority of people in Asia was largely Buddhist. The tribes of central Tibet, however, remained shamanist. "Shamanism" refers to a complex of ecstatic techniques guiding the shaman or sorcerer's ascent or descent to the sky or underworld, and the shaman's magical manipulation of elements and control of spirits. Shamanic practices and beliefs are found all over the world, and are generally associated with tribal society. Elements of them are evident in the "higher" supranational religions as well. Tibetan shamanism later developed into the system called *Bön* (pronounced "pern").[2]

The warlike Tibetan tribes united under a series of kings and became at times the dominant military power of Central Asia. They cast the shadow of their presence well beyond Tibet's modern confines. Having conquered what was to become eastern and western Tibet, their armies invaded Burma and Nepal (in A.D. 640), the Ganges Valley (A.D. 648), and waged frequent warfare with China, overrunning the Chinese capital in 763, and for a century seizing the strategic Central Asian oases on the silk road connecting China with the West (776–848). From these incursions the Tibetans returned, in shamanic style, with captured gods. But in addition, their contacts with more advanced peoples and the exigencies of administering their territories caused a rapid evolution of Tibetan culture. Among their captives were many Central Asian and Chinese Buddhist monks, while others were invited from India. A written language was developed, patterned on a Kashmiri or Central Asian Sanskrit, both for military-administrative purposes and the translation of Buddhist texts. Power came to be centralized in the King, superseding the council of nobles, in which he had been considered politically the "first among equals." Buddhism, with its concept of the "righteous King," provided the ideological basis for unity of the people under a centralized government.[3]

This Early Spread (sngar-dar) of Buddhism in Tibet evoked resistance from the established shamanic powers. A number of scriptures were translated from Sanskrit and Chinese under royal patronage. The diffusion occurred in part underground—the books and images having to be secreted at times in caves, or buried in the earth—for the shamanic ministers took fierce exception to this challenge, and called upon the local spirits to incite earthquakes, hailstorms, and epidemics. Indian scholars who had been invited by the King were forced to desist from their activities and to leave the country. In 747 the King secretly sent for the Kashmiri tantric adept (siddha) Padmasambhava, "Lotus-Born," to whom is credited the formal establishment of Buddhism in Tibet.

It is recorded in history that Padmasambhava made his way to Lhasa from Nepal, subdued the local deities who attacked him along the way, and forced them to vow to defend the new faith. He helped found the first religious establishment, designed on the model of the Mount Meru world system—one huge central temple surrounded by four "continents" and their satellite islands. The Indian pandits returned, and seven Tibetans were ordained there as monks. Intensive programs of instruction in Ch'an (the Chinese predecessor of Japanese "Zen"), tantric meditation, and scriptural translation were inaugurated. The Old Translation School (rnying-ma-pa) dates from this Early Spread.

After these years of success the Indian philosopher Śāntarakṣita, who acted as the first abbot of the monastic establishment, died from a kick of a horse. Without him the harmonious balance of the different schools was upset, and partisanship developed among the Buddhists. The Chinese monks made great strides in converting the populace; included among their patrons were several high ladies of the court. The party of Indian-oriented scholars appealed to the King (a third group, the tantric yogis, seem to have tried to avoid the issue), and the monarch sponsored a debate in about 792.

At issue was the relative validity of the "sudden" and "gradual" paths to enlightenment, associated with the Ch'an and Indian parties, respectively. The former taught intense meditation as a rapid means of cutting off discursive thought; the latter emphasized study and moral practice over a longer period for what they maintained were more profound and permanent results. The Indian party was upheld. From this time Indian Buddhism became the official doctrine of Tibet: The nation gradually lost its imperialistic and warlike ways.[4]

The chief spokesman for the Indian party, Śāntarakṣita's disciple Kamalaśīla, was murdered soon afterward. His death is traditionally blamed on the Chinese, however this may reflect the later anti-Chinese bias of Tibetans. Modern scholars now tend to consider Kamalaśīla's murder the work of the shamanist ministers of Bön, for the reasons that, following the debate of 792, Bön as well as Ch'an had been proscribed by the King, and the method of murder was shamanist in character. Kamalaśīla's kidneys were pressed until his death ensued, a mode used to avoid antagonizing the earth spirits with spilled blood.

In 842, by assassinating the King, the shamanist faction again gained control of the state and a reactionary persecution nearly wiped out Buddhism. Within a few years the Tibetan Empire, riven by petty rivalries and dissension, finally collapsed. The nation entered its Dark Ages.

The Doctrine of Indian Buddhism lay hidden and dormant until it was revived in the tenth and eleventh centuries in western Tibet. Eager students carried gold down to Indian masters, while yogis and scholars climbed the mountains into Tibet. But this Later Spread was not, like the former, a missionary tour for a world-mastering document. Buddhism in India was being overshadowed by brahmanical (Hindu) systems, and its existence was threatened by the terrible menace of iconoclastic Muslim invaders from the west.

Within two centuries the followers of this gentle faith, so vulnerably attached to their collections of books and artwork, who so often in history have proven helpless before those who contend with the sword, were to see Buddhism destroyed in India. The pandits of this age came to Tibet to seek refuge. They brought with them their wisdom and learning, and their secret tantric systems, and the enthusiastic Tibetans have developed and preserved them until modern times.

Three "reformed" schools of Tibetan Buddhism emerged from the spiritual renaissance of the eleventh century. The Tibetan schools are loosely identified by the color of their dress: The non-Buddhist Bön are black; the Old Translation School (rnying-ma-pa) are red; and the three new schools —Gelug, Kagyu, and Sakya—are yellow, white, and mixed.[5] The latter are "mixed" because their leaders may be either lay or monastic. The latter three schools are in that same order more or less strongly influenced by the great Indian missionary Atīśa, who resided in Tibet until his death in 1054. The spiritual system of the game Rebirth, with its clear division of the Buddhist vehicles—greater and lesser, sutra and tantra—is clearly based on the system imparted by Atīśa to the Tibetans in his monumental work, *The Lamp of the Enlightenment Path.*[6]

☞ II ☜

SAKYA PANDITA AND
THE INVENTION OF THE GAME

The game of Rebirth is a product of one of the Tibetan schools of the Later Spread. The creator of Rebirth was a member of the Sakya sect. The monastic center of Sakya was founded in 1073. The sect derives its system of basic texts and secret precepts, known as "the path and its fruit," from

Plate A. Sakya Pandita

India via the pilgrim-scholar Drog-mi. From Drog-mi's disciples these teachings have been passed down in the same family to the present members of the Sakya ruling house.

By Sa-pan's (Sa-skya paṇḍita [abbreviated Sa-pan]) time (1182–1251) the last Indian teachers had reached Tibet, in flight from the Muslim invasions, while the last intrepid Tibetan students still made their way down to the monastic universities of Bihar on the plains of central India. Sa-pan was learned in Sanskrit, as his name "pandit of the Sakyas" implies, and a master of all the Buddhist and Indian arts and sciences, not limited to scripture but including grammar, debate, medicine, astrology, and poetry. He was especially interested in the latest intellectual currents that flowed from India. He had intended to journey there but his uncle, who was also his monastic superior, forbade him. Sa-pan's compatriot, a monk named Dharmasvāmin, has left the poignant account of his own journey through the Indian heartland of Buddhism, ravaged by bands of Turkish soldiers, the devotees massacred or scattered. Dharmasvāmin returned very ill from the plague, and Sa-pan expressed his humble appreciation of his exploits.[7]

The closest Sa-pan came to India was Kyirong, now fifty miles north of Kathmandu in Nepal. In that place were active six Hindu teachers who had penetrated the spiritual barriers placed centuries before along the southern border passes to keep out non-Buddhists. These Hindus, it is said, caused disturbances in the local monasteries with their skill in debate. According to the account attributed to Sa-pan, he defeated and made Buddhist monks of them. Although the number six is suspiciously identical to the number of classical Hindu schools, the tale is not unreasonable; Sa-pan was known for his skill in logic. Although Sa-pan's orientation as a Sanskritist and Buddhist scholar was naturally toward India, his travels took him northward. His fame rests chiefly on a reluctant journey to Mongolia, and he is credited by the Mongolians with converting them to Buddhism and civilizing their manners.

This ironical outcome of Sa-pan's life derives from a circumstance of history. In 1207 the various secular and religious powers of Tibet had sent a delegation to submit themselves to Genghis Khan, whose armies were in the process of conquering the world up to the borders of Europe. This sensible action by the Tibetans spared them the unhappy fate of the other peoples who resisted Genghis' forces. After Genghis' death in 1227, various Tibetan nobles began to neglect the yearly tribute that had been negotiated, and, as a result, in 1239 Genghis' grandson Godan sent troops into Tibet; a monastery and several villages north of Lhasa were sacked. The Tibetan leaders turned to Sa-pan to represent them and negotiate a truce, as his reputation for holiness and rectitude was unparalleled. Godan commanded Sa-pan to his camp, and Sa-pan proceeded to Mongolia, turning the journey into a missionary tour that lasted a period of two years.

The reasons for Godan's summons are difficult to determine from the histories. Mongol and Tibetan accounts portray him as a King who was troubled by his own ignorance and sought illumination from the famous saint. Suggestions have also been made that he was seeking a cure for leprosy or, more plausibly, that like other Mongol chieftains, his curiosity was aroused by the diverse religious groups—Buddhist, Nestorian, Christian, Muslim, and Taoist—that had suddenly fallen under his sway. Other Khans are known to have sponsored grand contests of magic and philosophy to test the different traditions.

Sa-pan submitted the Tibetans to Godan Khan and was made viceroy in return. Thus the Sakya family began their reign over Tibet that lasted for three quarters of a century. They combined religious and secular sovereignty in their capital and unified the nation for the first time since the early empire.

In his famous letter to the Tibetan-speaking peoples, Sa-pan explained the situation, stating, in effect: "Godan has become a Dharma king. He favors me above all other teachers. I have joined Tibet to his confederation in return for personal sovereignty. Furthermore, other nations have suffered greatly by refusing the Mongol levies, so the petty princes of Tibet have no choice but to be grateful to me for this action and to keep their commitments as allies of the Mongols."

The other religious schools were not persecuted, as the Mongol ruler would ordinarily have done after favoring one among them, because of Sa-pan's own tolerance. As the power of the Mongols began to wane, the Sakyas were superseded by the other sects. But the pattern the Sakyas established of religious rule bolstered by foreign power set the pattern for Tibetan government until recent times.

Sa-pan's two young nephews had preceded him to the camp of Godan Khan. One of them, Pag-pa, was later destined (at age eighteen) to become Imperial Preceptor of Kublai's court in China, and was given Tibet as payment for the Emperor's first initiation into tantric Buddhism.[8]

Sa-pan left behind a corpus of 114 literary works. Coming at the close of the age of translators, he used his linguistic talents less in translation work than in commentaries and original contributions. He may be said to have completed the Sanskritization of the Tibetan language.

In Sa-pan's day Buddhism became more than an Indian import; the Dharma was finally assimilated into Tibetan thought and life. After centuries of devoted study and translation, original authors and commentators began to emerge. The Old Translation School evolved the genre of "rediscovered texts" (gter-ma), supposedly buried at the time of the Early Spread. Atīśa himself initiated this trend by discovering some scrolls from the Early Spread in an ancient temple. Whatever the origin of these texts —Tibetan scholars themselves have described some as having been forged or at least greatly edited—they served the purposes of bringing the tradition up to date and reforming it in a language clearly distinct from the style of Sanskrit translations. The great Kagyu yogis, Milarepa, "Crazy Drub-pa," and others, wrote of their experiences in the song and epic prose style of the popular literature—most significantly, in the colloquial language.[9]

In contrast with this, Sa-pan and later literateurs (the fifth Dalai Lama, for example) remolded their language along the lines of Sanskrit, which necessitated the very creation of Tibetan written language. Only in the later period, however, was the *kāvya*, "high poetry," of India extensively translated. Sa-pan was skilled in compositions that are so like the flowery verse of Indian poems that he has been unfairly accused by Western scholars of plagiarism. Not only the content and imagery but the elaborate style and Sanskritic compounds as well represent the complete absorption of the Indian literary style.

Sa-pan not only preserved the forms and wisdom of Indian Buddhism; he also expanded and evolved concepts and new modes in the same style that had not had the opportunity to develop in India because of social discord. In this sense Tibetan tradition on the most erudite levels may be said to have preserved the medieval Indian world view, not in the sense of sterile copying, but in a mastery of it such that it became a part of the living tradition. The game he invented is an example of this creative evolution of new forms in the Tibetan context.

☞ III ☜

THE GAME OF REBIRTH: ORIGINS AND DEVELOPMENT

SA-PAN'S GAME

Sa-pan's original version of the game exists as a blockprint, eight squares by nine.[10] (See Plate B.) The carving of the letters, lines, and ornamentation of the blockprint is a model of the scholarly precision for which the Sakyas are known. At the top are carved five verses, with two more below, describing the game. They are written in the ornamental style.

Verse I: After doing homage to Mañjuśrī, Bodhisattva of learning and wisdom and Sa-pan's special patron (here in his orange form, holding five arrows[11]), Sa-pan states his purpose in creating the game. Verse II: He says that most living beings find themselves neurotic[12] and helpless. Continually dissatisfied, tossed by the waves of birth and death, and without the leisure or opportunity for the Doctrine, they build up only the karmic causes of further strife and hardship. Verse III: Therefore in playing this educational game they may become certain as to the effects of vicious and virtuous activity. It will then be possible for them to create good karma and im-

Plate B. The Original Game of Rebirth

prove their situation. Verse IV: Sa-pan mentions the various cosmological systems and paths on the board, which are essentially the ones found in the present edition—he describes the squares as "the path to the pacification of existence." Verse V: Tokens should be used to mark the karmic progress of each player and should be arranged on Square 1. Then the die should be cast with a fierce oath "whose content is an imagined prayer to the Precious Three (the Buddha, his Doctrine, and the Buddhist Community)."

The two verses below state the moral of the game—one's lot in life will improve through the tradition of the profound and oceanic Doctrine—and praise the possible states of attainment found on the board.

Sa-pan's is a primitive form of the game. The layout resembles a tree. The central row of squares is the trunk, descending from Square 1 (Jambu Island, the earth) into *bardo,* the "intermediate" state between death and rebirth, down to the ghosts and the lowest hell. From Jambu Island one may rise quickly upward by casting four "one"s in a row, via the tantric path to Dharmabody, the winning square. This tantric path is much faster and easier than that of the modern game.

The twentieth-century version has abandoned this simpler structure in favor of greater depth and sophistication. The present game is faster-moving and more varied in possibilities than Sa-pan's original; it has thirty-two additional squares although half as many hells.

BHUTANESE VERSION

The modern Bhutanese game (Plate C) adds a new element: thirteen final stages leading to Buddhahood at the top. It has a very heavy tantric emphasis, and by contrast represents the mainstream of Tibetan cosmology, deriving more directly from Sa-pan's original. The Bhutanese version shows one elaboration frequently found in this type of game but not present in the modern edition: Along the bottom of the board, the six syllables of the die are correlated with those of the mantra Oṁ-ma-ṇi-pad-me-hūṁ, the sacred syllables of Avalokiteśvara, Bodhisattva of Compassion and patron deity of Tibet. These syllables stand, in the tantric tradition, for the six karmic destinations, god, asura, human, animal, hungry ghost, and hell being.

This correlation is not used in the present game, which places the human realm above that of the asuras. Nor will it work for Sa-pan's original. Neither the letters of the present game nor those of Sa-pan's have any

Plate C. A Modern Bhutanese Game of Rebirth

special meaning. However, the six sacred syllables are sometimes inscribed on special dice and used for children's versions of the game.[13]

NEPALESE VERSION

A variant of Rebirth from nineteenth-century Nepal (Plate D) presents the titles of the squares in Sanskrit as well as Tibetan. Much like the Bhutanese game in structure, it has undoubtedly derived from Sa-pan's prototype. This version represents a characteristically Nepalese fusion of Sanskrit with Tibetan elements. But whereas in the Middle Ages Nepalese Bud-

Plate D. A Modern Nepalese Game of Rebirth

dhism was translated from Sanskrit into Tibetan, here the process is reversed, Tibetan culture being the source of a Sanskrit artifact.

KOREAN GAME

A Korean game of this type, with 169 (13 by 13) squares, uses the six-syllable mantra on the die. Some of the names of the squares are in Sanskrit, but most are in Chinese; the game almost certainly came from China. No Chinese model is known, but there exist other Chinese and Korean games which, like the Japanese game soguroku, map a journey between two points. In a Chinese-Korean game called "the promotion of officials," dating from the Mongol Dynasty (1368–1644), the players make their way through the state bureaucracy from student to Grand Secretary, or through such specialized paths as doctor or astrologer. This game is complicated by the use of several dice, either four- or six-sided, and by the exchange of tokens or money.[14]

* * *

These East Asian games are undoubtedly specialized versions of some earlier type, perhaps of Sa-pan's game of Rebirth. Traditions concerning soguroko associate its origins with Central Asia and India.[15] Perhaps this sort of journey game entered the Chinese Empire via the Mongolians from Tibet. The origins and diffusion of games is a thorny and unrewarding problem. The thesis that board games in general were originally played with dice is fairly well established. In the case of chess, which seems to have come from seventh-century India, the cast of the die determined the type of piece to be moved.[16] Such board and dice games are quite ancient, dating at least as far back as the third century B.C. In the Pāli canon the Buddha includes such games among a list of eighteen recreations in which "certain recluses and Brahmans" indulge "while living on food provided by the faithful."[17]

How closely Sa-pan himself may have adhered to a previous model is impossible to determine. However a Hindu equivalent published in 1975 (the prototype of the English "Snakes and Ladders") shows a surprising coincidence with his: seventy-two squares. The published version has been modernized and is therefore difficult to date. It postdates Śaṁkara's synthesis of Hindu philosophy in the eighth or ninth centuries. In its allusion to Buddhism as "wrong intellect"—that is to say, nihilism, leading to "nullity"[18]—it follows the critique of that clever and able philosopher. Possibly Sa-pan took his inspiration from the Hindus encountered at Kyirong, or his game may have been copied by the Hindus on their return to India from Tibet.

Board games in general arise during medieval and later stages of cultural history, at a point when the doctrines that form the basis of any given society have thoroughly permeated the social fabric. The social ideology then seeks new and more imaginative forms of expression, and prephilosophic practices rise to the surface. Games, which are essentially re-creations of magical rites and divination procedures, come to be devised around secular concepts, such as warfare, capitalism, or religious doctrines.

> Based upon certain fundamental conceptions of the universe, (games) are characterized by a certain sameness, if not identity, throughout the world. Without the confirmation of linguistic evidence they are insufficient to establish the connection of races or the transference of culture. They furnish, however, the most perfect existing evidence of the underlying foundation of mythic concepts upon which so much of the fabric of our culture is built. . . .[19]

This association of games with older practices has led one writer to misidentify Rebirth as a divination board. Evidently not having consulted a Tibetan, the writer speculates that it was used to divine the future state of one recently dead, or even to determine the appropriate ceremonies.[20] Such a form of divination would contradict the most basic Buddhist doctrine: One can certainly learn to recollect past lives, but to predict the future would be impossible for ordinary people, since it will be what they make of it through their actions, their karma.

Nonetheless, the game is in some way connected to a desire to foresee the future, at least in its potential. This primeval longing for prescience has been diverted into an educational device and tool for mindfulness. In this way it parallels the widespread adoption into the fold of the Dharma of astrology, divination, and magical manipulation, which as Buddhist arts are largely a product of its later tantric period.

*   *   *

Like games and other worldly pursuits, astrology and divination are far from the core of Buddhist practice in all periods, being associated with the striving for mundane success, especially since they reinforce the delusion of a stable and permanent "self." In the Pāli canon the Buddha advises his students:

> In these ways he is not wisely attending: If he thinks, "Did I exist in the past? Did I not exist in the past? What was I in the past? What was I like in the past? Will I exist in the future? Will I not exist in the future? What will I be in the future? Having become that, what [else] will I become in the future?" To one who pays unwise attention in these ways, one of the six [wrong] views arise: "There is for me a self" —the view arises to him as though it were true, as though it were real. . . .[21]

Buddhism teaches the illusion of selfhood to be the primary cause of suffering, and then shows the means to liberation. To speculate as to one's future state is thus counterproductive to spiritual work. Such prognostication as is practiced in the Pāli texts is generally done by brahmanas, such as the seer (rishi) who examines the infant Buddha and, from physical signs, predicts his conquest of the world. In one long passage on moral conduct, the Buddha specifically counsels his disciples against earning their livelihood, "like certain recluses and Brahmans," by the practice of "low arts" such as palmistry, divining by omens and signs, by bird and animal cries, auguries and celestial portents, interpreting dreams, making charms and mantras, and so forth.[22]

This very statement nonetheless indicates that just such "low arts" were practiced by non-Buddhist holy men from the earliest period; it was only a matter of time before they would be absorbed into the Dharma. Without them, Tibetan religion would have been greatly impoverished.

In the Mahāyāna tradition emphasis is placed not only on the spiritual progress of the individual, but also on the duty of the bodhisattva to help others. He leads them toward Awakening (bodhi) and meets their more immediate needs as well. Worldly arts and sciences are seen as legitimate means to both these ends. Astrology is included, along with medicine and poetry, among the subsidiary vidyās of his repertoire, but it is still extracanonical and secondary to the aims of the religious system.

Later, as Buddhism became overly scholastic and somewhat removed in its concerns from the community of lay supporters, it was regenerated by the infusion of tantric and other popular influences. Buddhist tantrism evolved from two major sources: the elaboration of meditational techniques common to the earlier schools, and the renewal of magical practices. Here the means becomes the end; the base and the divine are commingled, the one supporting the other. The appeal of tantra lay in its use of the desire for prescience and power not as subsidiary aids and means of conversion, but as the potential for such desires to become the goal itself through a yogic transmutation.

The latest period of Buddhism in India saw a partial rapproachement, in practice if not in theory, with the Hindu Śaivite tantric texts. Here prognostication and magical practices became increasingly important. In about the tenth century the "Wheel of Time" (Kālacakra) tantra appeared, being introduced soon after into Tibet. The Kālacakra is the most important tantric cycle in Tibet, coming at the head of the "tantric" section of the sacred canon.[23] As its name implies, it deals specifically with astrology. This subject is still taught as the second year of Tibetan medical training: In the tantric world view the structure of the microcosm—the individual personality—mirrors that of the macrocosm—the universe itself.

Another tantra to reach Tibet at this time is one of the sources of the Kālacakra, entitled the "Rising Song" (Svarodaya) tantra, "victorious in war."[24]

Such texts reflect the anxiety felt by Buddhists and others in southern and central Asia for the future of their civilization. The Kālacakra predicts the appearance of a great king, from the mythical land of Shambhala, who will defeat the Turkish Muslims and return Buddhism to pre-eminence.[25] There are discussions in it of military tactics such as bombardment, magic arrows, and fires, and the evocation of windstorms, many of which were used in this century, with obvious lack of success, against British and Chinese invaders of Tibet.[26]

Tibetans have in addition their own widespread and ancient traditions of divinatory and magical techniques that predate the introduction of Buddhism. There are texts from the ninth century describing divination by lightning and by the calls of birds. Several systems of astrology, the earliest coming from China in the seventh century, have by now been combined into the complex formulae that the government astrologers used to devise the yearly calendar and almanac. Techniques of divination range from the complex rituals used by professional and state oracles down to practices as simple as our flipping of a coin. Numerology is common: For example, numbered arrows will be shaken in a quiver until one or several fall out, the numbers being used to determine the results. Dice are also thrown, and a book is consulted on the meaning of the numbers that result. Dice boards are used to answer questions relating to this life.[27]

Such is the context in which the game of Rebirth appears. Yet Rebirth was widely played even in the strictest monasteries, which made no common practice of coercive magic or divination. Although it might be suggested that the game is by its nature associated with such low arts, and that it implicitly reinforces the notion that a "self" is fated to be reborn in the various states depicted (these criticisms would seem not at all inappropriate to an educated Tibetan), one should be reminded that it is after all a game—an educational device to make one mindful of the possible fruits of one's actions.

☞ IV ☜

KARMA AND REBIRTH:
THE PHILOSOPHIC BASIS

The game we call Rebirth bears the more elaborate title "Determination of the Ascension of Stages."[28] By rolls of the die one maps out the course of one's future rebirths or, more optimistically, the stages of one's progress toward Awakening.

The board has a certain number of semimythic geographic places, such as the four continents that surround the great world mountain, Meru, magical lands that can be located at various points on the earth, as well as "Hinduism" and "barbarism" associated with India and Central Asia.

The Tibetans show a lively appreciation for geography in other contexts. On the popular level they considered themselves—as have other peoples—the center of the world. Central Tibet, the legend goes, was at one time a vast sea. Later it was covered with lakes and forests, and as these diminished in size, the monkey inhabitants evolved into human beings. The Tibetan people were generated from the union of the male and female bodhisattvas, Avalokiteśvara and Tārā, in the guises of a monkey and a rock demoness. Their offspring founded the first village. In historical times (from the seventh century), Tibet was perceived to be surrounded by China to the east, India to the south, Persia and Rome-Byzantium to the west, the Turks and others to the north. Associated with these four regions are, respectively, divination and technology, philosophy, wealth, and horses with the implements of war. Some Tibetans considered themselves the savage north, and India the center of the world. Modern Tibetans have evolved a science of geography that encompasses the earth from China to the Americas—most of the information coming from China—but with special emphasis on pilgrimage routes in Asia.[29]

This game is certainly not a geography in either the scholarly or the popular sense. Certain squares can be loosely identified with lands of the Orient or even the West, yet the game must be said to present states of mind and spirit. The "places" represented derive largely from the cosmological conceptions of Indian Buddhism.

In its structure, Rebirth is highly sophisticated; the fifteen-hundred-year course of Buddhism in India witnessed several cosmologic systems develop and overlay one another. Tibetan modifications are also evident at several points.

THE WHEEL OF LIFE

The fundamental conceptions of the Indo-Tibetan world view are incorporated into a chart of the Wheel of Life (Plate E), which is used to illustrate the functioning of karma and the process of continuing rebirth. The Wheel of Life is a picture of sàmsāra, the world of birth and death; in it the myriads of living beings are classified in five types, each demonstrating a state of mind that has given rise to that type. It depicts the renewal of existence in twelve symbolic pictures around its edge.

The cycle of birth and death, sàmsāra, is painted between the jaws of Māra, lord of this realm, here symbolizing impermanence. Within the spokes of the wheel are represented the five major karmic destinations: Two above, three below. The higher destinies are god, asura, and human beings. The happiest state is that of the devas, gods of the world of sense desire, whose lives are continual pleasure and sensual delight mitigated only by the fact that they must eventually die and pass to another state. Their exalted station is the reward of generosity and moral conduct.

Included with these gods are the asuras, or "jealous gods." They are very powerful and have as much reason to be happy as the gods, but are

Plate E. The Wheel of Life

consumed with anger and envy, and are sometimes classed among the demons for this reason. They are shown in battle with the devas. Like the Greek Titans they were expelled from heaven. The story goes that the gods first got them drunk, then overpowered them. The two groups are at war—the issue symbolized by the wish-granting tree, whose fruit is whatever one may desire. The tree has its roots in the realm of the asuras (square No. 15 on the game board), but flowers in the heaven of the thirty-three gods (square No. 28). The asuras periodically attempt to claim the fruits and are just as often defeated—for the gods with their karmic legacy of generosity and pure moral conduct are much stronger. The asura state is the result of liberality mixed with quarreling and violence.

To the right of the gods is the human condition, with all its ups and downs. Men and women are shown in their daily activities—keeping a household, bearing children, and practicing religion. In terms of spiritual possibility this is the luckiest rebirth. The lower states are too concerned with pain and survival to think of enlightenment. Asuras are too full of anger, devas too self-satisfied. The human condition is characterized by striving, either for worldly or spiritual aims, that results from the illusion of the subject-object duality.

At the bottom of the wheel are the three unhappy destinies: animals, ghosts, and hells. Lowest of these are the hell worlds, the karmic result of sustained malicious activity. The hells are various, and, as in Dante's *Inferno*, tailored to the nature of the criminal. But there is one fundamental difference from the Christian concept: The hells are no more permanent than anything else in the world. Hell beings await the exhaustion of their karma, not an external redeemer. Their state resembles the Christian purgatory, in which vicious habits are burned away. Above the hells to the right are hungry ghosts (pretas). These creatures are hungry and thirsty, but their necks are the size of pins, their bellies like hills, and food turns to fire in their mouths. Their senses are completely distorted by greed. Across from them are the animals of the sea, land, and air, including insects. Their misfortune is to be born so stupid—the result of willful ignorance—that in general they have no aim in life but to follow their physical instincts or to be tamed and subservient to others.

Each of these types of creatures is served by a great compassionate bodhisattva, who takes a form most appropriate for communicating with him.

At the gateway to the hells is the court of Yama, Lord of the Dead, flaming in his wrath. He symbolizes the mechanism of karmic judgment and rebirth. He holds up the mirror of karma before those confronting him after death, shows them what they have made of themselves, and sends them on their way. Creatures in this intermediate state then circle through the various destinies to seek an appropriate birth, rising up the light side, if they have engaged in some spiritual practice, or back down the dark into hell.

The Buddha is pointing his disciple to the legend (top left) as the alternative to sàmsāra. The verses read:

> You should begin, you should cast off,
> Set forth in the Buddhist teaching!
> Like an elephant in a reed hut,
> Conquer the Lord of Death's legion!

> Anyone vigilant enough,
> By practicing Dharma training,
> Will abandon the round of rebirth
> And make an end of suffering.

At the hub of the wheel are pictured three animals which represent the motivating forces: the rooster of passion, the snake of malice, and the pig of ignorance. These are the root causes of sàmsāra.

Around the rim is depicted the mechanism of karma and rebirth, twelve symbolic illustrations of links of the chain of interdependent origination. The chain is conceived as circular: It represents sàmsāra; it has no beginning, and only by breaking it does one make an end. Its comprehension is the content of the great Awakening and freedom from the necessity of an otherwise endless series of rebirths.

With *ignorance* as the root cause, pictured at the top as a blind man heading directly toward a precipice (the first link of the chain of interdependent origination), and *karmic formations,* depicted by a potter molding pots (second link),'we have the conditions that have given rise to this life. Ignorance or confusion regarding the true nature of reality, especially the common delusion of the "selfhood," which needs to be fed by a separate external reality, has given rise to karma: "activity" of body, speech, and mind. Like the clay pot, we and the conditions of our lives are molded by habitual actions, which leave mental impressions as seeds to develop into future states of existence.

Karmic potentialities give rise to *consciousness,* represented as a restless monkey rushing about the house (third link). Consciousness, bearing tendencies from the past, is reborn. The Buddhists speak of "rebirth" rather than "reincarnation" to avoid giving the false impression that some "entity" enters a "body" to be reborn. Rather, the body is created by a karmic impetus from the past. The consciousness that is reborn can no more be isolated as a "thing" than can a fire spreading from tree to tree. The fire does not exist without heat, air, and fuel; ordinary consciousness is a result of causes and conditions that have been created by ignorant activity in past lives. Thus we enter the present life in accord with previous thoughts and deeds.

The mental seeds sown by past karma, working through the present consciousness, give rise to *name and form*—that is, the psychophysical organism, the spiritual and physical elements that constitute personality. This is represented as two men in a boat (fourth link).

Based on name and form are the *six senses,* including mind (fifth link) —a house with six windows open, but still vacant, for nothing yet has entered from outside. The five senses are ready to grasp external objects. The sixth sense is mind in its functions of perceiving mental phenomena (for example, memory) and of analyzing the data of the five physically based senses and turning them into perceptions. Here exist the means to grasp the external world.

Without the six senses there would be no *contact* with objects of sense: depicted by a human couple embracing (sixth link). Without contact, there is no *sensation:* an arrow in the eye (seventh link). These are the effects in this life of ignorance and past karma. Then follow the present causes of future rebirth.

Dependent on sensation is thirst or *desire:* a person drinking (eighth link). From desire comes *grasping:* plucking fruit from a tree (ninth link). From grasping emerges *becoming,* depicted by pregnancy (tenth link). From these causes in the present life comes *rebirth:* a woman giving birth (eleventh link). Of course, without birth there would be no great aggregate of pain, old age, illness, and *death:* a corpse being carried to the fire (twelfth link).

These twelve links form a circular chain covering past, present, and future lifetimes—past causes (links 1 and 2), present results (3, 4, 5, 6, and 7), present causes (8, 9, and 10), and the next life (11 and 12). This is the cycle without beginning of birth, death, and rebirth; it is the explanation of our existence and our suffering as the result of a set of twelve causes and conditions. Furthermore, when the individual is understood to be the result of these karmic causes and conditions, one is seen to have no "self," no permanent and immutable reality in himself.

Sexuality is not considered a root cause of suffering, despite the sexual imagery in this scheme. In Buddhism it is not necessarily tied to procreation. Other types of birth are recognized, such as the "miraculous" creation of the gods. Sexual pleasure is one of the great pastimes of the gods, yet they do not reproduce by fornication, and they are considered to attain satisfaction much more quickly, easily, and repeatedly than do human beings. In the Buddhist view there is no harm in pleasure; it is confused striving and grasping that create the conditions for further suffering. Sexuality is considered an attendant condition of suffering. When associated with the wrong view—seeking permanence in the transient—it constitutes one of the circumstances of human misery. The only secure refuge from suffering is to be found in direct confrontation with realities of existence and the essentially empty nature of the human organism. By understanding completely the fact of birth and death as a chain of interdependent causes, one is enabled to transcend the process and to leave the realm of karmic necessity, in fact, to truly experience the fullness of life.[30]

* * *

This explanation for the generation of the living organism is clearly in conflict with materialistic theories that regard consciousness as no more than a function of material elements. The Buddhist view presupposes that consciousness or Mind, in the process of moving from one life to the next, can exist independently of a physical basis. Mind, the traditional argument goes, cannot arise from material sources, since these have a different nature. Knowledge—for example, memory—arises as dependent on the continuum of previous mental states. Prior experience results in later knowledge. Life is thus a series of mental states. Furthermore, if Mind were dependent on body, it would increase and decrease in vitality with the growth and decline of the body, and might even exist in a corpse, since the physical basis is present.

The body is admittedly a co-operating cause for the functioning of thought. But, it is argued, the union of sperm and egg that produces the physical constituents of being does not suffice to explain the resultant child's attitudes and mental abilities. If it did, then an intelligent child could not be born to dull parents. Innate knowledge and instincts can only be reasonably explained as the fruits of karmic heredity. Finally, the non-perception of something, in this case the nonmemory of past lives, is no proof of its nonexistence, especially when compared with the reports of those experienced in mental concentration who remember their own past lives, as well as occasional incidents of such memory in young children.[31]

The existence of the material world, relative to mind, is not a major issue in this central thesis of Buddhism. In the Vehicle of the Disciples, corresponding to the philosophically more primitive Buddhist view, the world is reduced to its component elements, dharmas, which are regarded as real. The enumeration of worldly dharmas varies slightly from school to school, consisting generally of the physical referents of sense impressions, as well as thoughts, feelings, perceptions, and karmic impulses.

For all the schools, the external world is of secondary importance where karmic theory is concerned. For karma, although it consists of actions of body, speech, and mind, is essentially a matter of intention: It is the mental event associated with an action that causes the impression resulting in conditions for the future. Furthermore, it is always the thought that motivates karmic activity; an accidental killing is not considered murder, but when one hires an assassin, although it is only a verbal action, it has the same karmic effect or worse than wielding the knife, for the intention is made manifest. One's karmic destiny is the result of a single forcible action, borne into the future as a seed implanted in deep layers of the mind, or of a habitual and ingrained attitude toward the world. At worst, attitudes of craving, malice, and bewilderment lead to the three states of woe: the ghostly, hellish, and animal destinies. Attachment to the Dharma creates merit, thus causing rebirth in conditions favorable to following the path. Combinations of good with bad karma lead to mixed results.

Karmic consequences are infinitely varied. The treatises describe the relative vitality of the external world, length of life, realms for collective activities such as warfare, and so forth. The reduction of life to six destinies is made for illustrative purposes only. That which distinguishes Buddhism from other religious traditions is precisely this theory of karma, and the reduction of life and the world to verifiable elements (dharmas).[32] The living organism is thus reborn in dependent origination on past karma and the elements of the world.

> That which befalls living beings is only the fruit of actions—
> wholesome and unwholesome—of body, speech, and mind,
> accomplished by themselves. There is no other Creator.[33]

26

In the Greater Vehicle, representing the more advanced philosophical stages of Buddhist thought, mundane dharmas are viewed as less important and less "real," for they are themselves the result of dependent origination. It is thus established that all phenomena—not merely the living person—originate in dependency on one another and have no essence or "self." There is no essence of "fire," only a set of conditions—heat, air, and fuel. Yet, even then, the view is not that the world is *māyā*, "illusion." Our experiences—rocks, trees, rivers, streets and buildings, pleasure and pain—are real, in the conventional sense of the term. They are the fruits of past action, and we participate in the present experience of them with all our being. The Awakened view is that our experience of the phenomenal world is "like an illusion, like a dream, like a magic show"—or, in modern terms, like a movie with which we may identify but that is, in reality, no more than a celluloid tape with a sound track.

Passing beyond the conventional understanding of "real"—our naked experience—we learn that things and events, perceptions and responses, even thoughts, which we ordinarily assume have some meaning and essential nature of their own, in actuality have none. These mental and physical dharmas that seem to be discrete phenomena, each with reality and characteristics all their own, derive meaning and value only from their interdependence. There is no edification in a movie that does not interact with the senses and mind of an audience.

Ordinarily we experience phenomena through the haze of attachment, aversion, and bewilderment. This is not to say that they are not real as experienced. But if "real" means "existing in itself" or "meaningful as it is," then their reality is empty, for they are real and meaningful only in context. No thing comes to exist apart from a complex of causes and conditions. And no thing remains forever. So nothing is real in itself, and nothing in the world should be relied upon as permanent.

Within the Greater Vehicle, the "Mind-only (Cittamātra) School takes to its logical conclusion the observation that karma is an essentially mental process. Basically, that view is that all phenomena represent the fruition of seeds that have been sown in the unconscious mind by past activity. So the only reality is Mind. Whether or not this view is more conducive to liberation, it is a logical extension of the theory of karmic causation. It still does not deny the relative reality of the external world, however, for internal and external events have the same level of reality. Both are essentially empty. There are three levels of truth in the Mind-only system: (1) As fabrications of mind, all things are *unreal*. (2) *Relative* to one another, they are *real*. Likewise, the process of rebirth, the functioning of mind as a storehouse of karmic seeds is *relatively real*. (3) Emptiness, as the abso· lute principle and essential nature of all phenomena, is *absolutely real*.

Buddhahood itself is seen by the Mind-only School as a seed lying dormant in the mind or in a state of development. As it develops, we come to understand the relative nature of self and the world, and passing from our illusions into the clear morning light of the great Awakening from suffering, the elements of self and the world will still be there—"like an illusion, like a dream."

* * *

In the scriptures and treatises on the workings of karma, on which the commentaries to the squares of this game are based, the focus is on activities done while in the human state, and the different states of rebirth that result from them.[34] Buddhist teachings are not unconcerned with the welfare of other classes of living beings. Frequently in the scriptures (sūtra) one encounters tales of nonhuman creatures, including accounts of their future rebirths. There is, for example, the generalization commonly made regarding the devas and higher divinities: Long-lived and comfortable as they may be, they cannot escape eventual dissolution—the "fall" of a god —and rebirth in another state in accord with karma maturing from previous lives. There are also the well-known jātaka tales, narrating past lives of the Buddha Śākyamuni and including many stories in which the protagonists are animals. But the treatises on karma, an important genre of Buddhist literature, are naturally directed to humanity, for among living beings only they have the leisure to read and study, and the impetus, provided by their unique mixture of pleasurable and painful experience, to attempt to transcend their condition.

The game of Rebirth is conceived on the model of the treatises on karma, beginning with the hells and working upward. The result of each cast of the die would normally be taken to reflect some human action, even if one is moving from one nonhuman state to another.

The game may be simplistically termed "moralistic," for the varieties of moral relationship between oneself and the world, as formulated in the Buddhist ethical code—the ten wholesome and ten unwholesome types of action—are the major causes of good and bad karmic destinies. But these are not the only causes reflected in the game. There are higher heavens of attenuated materiality that are the results of meditative trances, and the

28

paths of various religious traditions combining moral practice, meditation, and study.

The game board, therefore, presents the possibilities inherent in our present human condition, and shows the traditional paths for wholesome development. Karma as "activity" encompasses all the activities of living beings. But our concern is primarily with the business of human beings, for the gods have little temptation either to stray from righteousness or to strive to improve their lot, whereas the lower orders of creatures are constrained by circumstance and temperament to instinctual reactions and the struggle for survival. Human beings are most capable of intentional and purposeful activity for good and bad aims, and it is to this issue that the treatises and this game direct our attention.

The law of karma is illustrated by a number of similes in Buddhist literature. Karmic process—deeds and their consequence—is like a monkey ceaselessly climbing and circling all the nooks and crannies in the forest. It resembles an actor with many roles, a fish in the flood of desire and, most of all, a painter creating forms and colors.[35] The karmic determination of one's present and future state is seen as the supreme act of imagination. Individually and collectively we are the painters of the canvas of the future.

The association of modes of consciousness with the painter's different colors is a literary and artistic motif that far predates the well-known formulation in the tantras. But in the tantric practices of visualization they take a dogmatic form: white for the gods, red for asuras, blue for humanity, green for animals, yellow for ghosts, and smoke-colored for the hells.[36]

The approach to Awakening brings one into association with the essential nature of thought, purified of karmic form and coloration and freed from the imaginative and falsely fabricating mind that turns the self and world into a dualistic maze of subject and object, fear and desire, a process of unity and alienation. Purified thought is described as an experience of clarity and radiance. This essential nature of mind—clarity and radiance—is shared by all living beings, from the lowest to the most spiritually advanced. The path to its realization is a matter of gradually purging the veils of illusion created by activity tinged with ignorance.

* * *

Karmic causation is the theoretical background for Buddhist ethics. The ordinary person will behave properly when aware of the consequences. The religious practitioner also has karmic consequences in mind, but has another reason as well: Morality, as a stable and wholesome attitude toward oneself and others, is a necessary precondition for meditative practice, which is in turn the basis of the understanding gained from study. So the three aspects of spiritual training—morality, meditation, and study—are supported each by the other as a house on its foundation.

Since karma is essentially intention, morality is the beginning of meditation. Learning to discipline the mind is thus the starting point of the religious path.

> If one wishes to further one's training,
> One firmly protects the mind;
> For if restless thought is not guarded,
> One's training cannot be nurtured.

> The damages done here,
> By a wild mad elephant
> Can't compare with those to be done in the hells,
> By the roaming bull of the mind.

> If one binds the bull of the mind
> With the rope of full mindfulness,
> There is no more reason for fear,
> And all wholesomeness comes to hand.[37]

The principles of morality are reduced into a list, as are most other aspects of Buddhism, for the purpose of memorization. The ten unwholesome actions are murder, theft, improper sexuality (the three of body), lying, harsh words, slander, gossip (the four of speech), covetousness, ill will, and wrong views (the three of mind). The ten virtuous actions are the abstention from each of the above, plus the appropriate positive substitutions. Karmic retributions take effect in the same life, the very next, or farther in the future.

Each action may be elaborated on in some detail. For example, murder is defined as "the act of cutting off the life force of another living being, with premeditation and awareness of the fact that the victim is alive." There are three degrees of gravity: murder of an arhat or other spiritually advanced being, of a religious practitioner in general (these two degrees not only deprive another of life but also hinder in general the chances of others for spiritual development), and ordinary murder of persons or animals.

Three *motives* for murder are recognized: greed (for example, the hunt), anger (as, for example, a trait of bad character), and intellectual error (as in killing animals for religious sacrifice). One may commit murder oneself or have it done by another; both are considered murder.

Mitigating circumstances: to kill ants while walking, for a physician to kill while attempting to cure, for parents to unwittingly kill while chastising their children, to kill insects by means of a fire. These are not murder if the intent to kill is not present. In this Buddhism differs from Jainism which takes karma not as intention but as a concrete property of the organism that needs to be expunged, and so attempts to avoid all harm to living beings—sweeping the path before one with a broom and breathing through a filter.

Aggravating circumstances: conspiracy to kill, taking satisfaction in the result (as in a hunt or a fight), the manufacture of arms, praising the act of killing (the merits of sacrifice to the gods, bravery of soldiers, or the glory of war). These attitudes constitute a worse form of murder since they incite others to do it, thus harming their spiritual growth.

Retributions for murder: plunging into the three lower destinies. If reborn in the human realm, one will have a short life span. In heaven or among the asuras, one will be exposed to the perils of warfare and possibly be killed.

The *virtuous action* corresponding to murder is the absence of hatred and the gift and protection of life. This is associated with the meditational series called "the four stations of brahma": friendliness, compassion, appreciation, and equanimity toward others. Its *retributions:* In the present life one is beautiful, rich, and noble; one lives a long, full life, protected by divinities. In the next life one may be born a Wheel-Turning King (Cakravartin), a huge and powerful asura or demigod sovereign, or even a lord of the gods, Brahmā, Indra, or Māra. If one takes the religious paths, the results are quick and sure.

"Improper sexuality" generally means adultery. By abstaining from it one is said to win the praises and confidence of all, and to have mates who are loyal and without jealousy. In one's next life one may be born in a heaven of sensual pleasure without, as is the case with other gods, being abandoned suddenly by one's consorts when the time of one's fall approaches.[38]

To aid mindfulness in moral conduct, vows are taken. The layperson takes vows to avoid the ten unwholesome actions. The monk or nun takes more complex vows—first as a novice, then as fully ordained—that regulate the entire conduct of life. The bodhisattva resolves to help all other living beings on the path to Awakening, with the ethical code attendant to this course. The tantric yogi, basing his vows on the bodhisattva vow, follows an extremely rigorous set of commitments regarding verbal and physical actions and attitudes of mind. All these vows are considered aids toward guarding the mind. They enable one, while following the path, to progress, as one does in the course of this game, into progressively more sublime and spiritual states.

☞ V ☜

OUTLINE OF THE GAME BOARD

OVERVIEW

The Tibetan Buddhist vision of the universe, comprising both saṁsāra and nirvana, is represented in outline by the squares of the board. The scheme of the game is in fact a combination of several overlapping systems. Beginning from the bottom are the regions of the world with its karmic destinies. From the fifth row upwards are the paths to Buddhahood. The aim in playing the game is to move from the degrading round of rebirth among the lower states, from hells to gods and back, into one of the paths of the Greater Vehicle—the Mahāyāna proper or its tantric subdivision—and to continue on it, past the irreversible stage, to the Dharma body of the Buddha. From there one performs the various tasks of the fully Awakened, gradually moving to nirvana, the top-left square.

Across the top of the board, three representations of the enlightenment principle oversee the progress of the game. At the left is Amitābha, Buddha of "boundless light," seated in meditation. At the right is Padmasambhava, "lotus born," the precious guru of Tibet who holds the trident, skullcup, and vajra thunderbolt of a tantric yogi. A stupa is at the

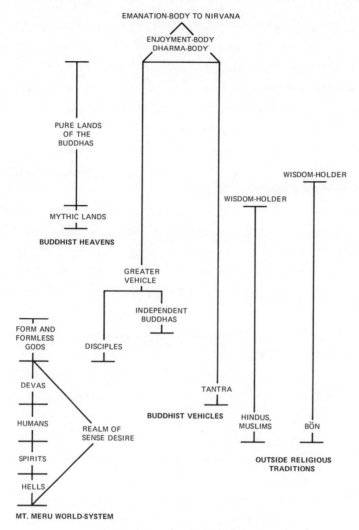

EMANATION-BODY TO NIRVANA

ENJOYMENT-BODY
DHARMA-BODY

PURE LANDS
OF THE
BUDDHAS

WISDOM-HOLDER

WISDOM-HOLDER

MYTHIC LANDS

BUDDHIST HEAVENS

GREATER
VEHICLE

INDEPENDENT
BUDDHAS

FORM AND
FORMLESS
GODS

DISCIPLES

DEVAS

TANTRA

HUMANS

REALM OF
SENSE DESIRE

BUDDHIST VEHICLES

HINDUS,
MUSLIMS

BÖN

SPIRITS

HELLS

**OUTSIDE RELIGIOUS
TRADITIONS**

MT. MERU WORLD-SYSTEM

Plate F. Map of the Game Board

center, depository of the indestructible relics of a Buddha who has reached nirvana and left the world.

If the various cosmological systems and spiritual paths were abstracted from the game, they could be depicted as in Plate F.

A.   THE THREE REALMS

The numeric progression of the rows is from right to left, ascending to the top of the board; those to the left and above being higher. Thus the upper levels represent increasing purification of the grosser elements of existence—attachment, aggression, and bewilderment—freedom from harm and violence, and latitude of lifestyle. Approaching liberation, the possibilities of physical form and activity, derived from one's meditative powers, become virtually unlimited.

The six karmic destinies are represented in the lower four rows of the board. Hells occupy the bottom rows; hungry ghosts, animals, and assorted demons the second. The third is occupied by human beings, except for their most powerful member and ideal ruler, the Wheel-Turning King (square No. 26), who is classed among the deva gods on the fourth row.

All this is considered the "Realm of Sense Desire" (kāma-dhātu). Here, creatures have a diversity of physical forms and their senses are possessed by the concerns of material objects. Their goals, their pleasure and pain are defined in terms of sensory stimulus and gross materiality.[39] There are two realms besides: that of Form (rūpadhātu) and the "Formless Realm" (arūpa-dhātu). These are shown in row five (square Nos. 35–37).

These two higher realms constitute levels of godhead beyond the devas of the Wheel of Life. These stations are not attained by generosity and pure morality, which grant one mastery of the Realm of Sense Desire, but by advanced degrees of meditation: the four trances (dhyāna) and the four equalizations (samāpatti).[40] These are stages of vastly extended consciousness and its transcendence.

The Realm of Form (square Nos. 35 and 37) has seventeen levels. The first three correspond to the first stage of trance, in which one-pointedness or concentration of mind is attained. The gods existing in this realm have diverse physical forms and unity of idea. They are one-pointed in their belief in a creator God. The Great Brahmā (Mahābrahmā) is the highest among them. He corresponds to the concept of God held by the practitioners of other religious traditions: God, the Omniscient, Creator, Overlord, Father of all.

This conception held by Mahābrahmā and his devotees is explained as a simple delusion: At the end of its previous age, the world was destroyed by wind and water up to the level of the higher gods of form. Afterward a god fell into the state of the Great Brahma gods. Being the first one there, he considered himself the only living being in the world, for there was as yet nothing beneath him, and even beings on his level cannot see those above. As others fell into this existence, he came to consider himself as their father and creator, and they, seeing that he had been there before, accepted this fiction as the gospel truth. As some among them fell into even lower states, they perpetuated the error. Eventually some were reborn as men. Retaining some of their previous meditative powers, they recollected having been gods in the retinue of Great Brahmā. These men became his priests (brāhmanas), initiating the worship of a father god— "The Creator is up there!" In the Buddhist view, as previously shown, the origin of the material elements of the world is unimportant. Creation is understood in terms of the karmic experience of its inhabitants.[41]

Above the Brahma gods are three levels called gods of light, all with radiant bodies. When the flames that destroy the world at the end of an age mount up to this level, certain younger gods are disturbed. Those who previously have lived through this destruction must assure these gods that only the palace of Brahmā below them will be destroyed. Thus they, unlike the Brahma gods, have a diversity of ideas. This is the state of the second trance.

Even higher are three types of splendid gods, the third trance. Since they enjoy the highest worldly happiness, they have a unity of perception.

In the highest reaches of the Realm of Form, the eight levels of the fourth trance, are the gods of the Pure Abode (square No. 37). Supreme among them is the Akaniṣtha heaven. Since the Formless Realm has no "place," the Akaniṣtha is the highest of the godly abodes. It is placed, however, not in the fifth row of the board but at the top (square No. 84), for the Akaniṣtha has been taken over by a later cosmological conception and made into the abode of a buddha. Therefore, the highest heaven of form is the supreme among god realms and buddha pure lands on the board.[42]

Above the Realm of Form, in terms of meditational progress, is the Formless Realm (square No. 36). These rebirths derive from four states called equalizations. With the first equalization, perceptions of form and materiality are transcended; one abides in pure and infinite consciousness. On the second level, consciousness is transcended; one abides in infinite space. The third transcends space, attaining the stage of "nothing at all." The last is termed "neither perception nor nonperception"; it represents the limit of sàmsāra, at which the yogi "touches nirvana with his body." The three realms of sàmsāra can be represented as a pyramid. (See Plate G.)

However, the pyramid is not a traditional representation of the three realms, and may be misleading in that the gods of the higher levels actually have more space with greater freedom of movement, larger bodies, and longer life spans than those of the lower realms. The traditional scheme, many elements of which are held in common with Hindu cosmology,

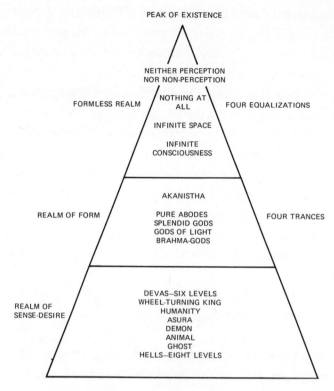

PEAK OF EXISTENCE

NEITHER PERCEPTION
NOR NON-PERCEPTION

NOTHING AT
ALL

FORMLESS REALM   INFINITE SPACE   FOUR EQUALIZATIONS

INFINITE
CONSCIOUSNESS

AKANISTHA

PURE ABODES
REALM OF FORM   SPLENDID GODS   FOUR TRANCES
GODS OF LIGHT
BRAHMA-GODS

DEVAS—SIX LEVELS
WHEEL-TURNING KING
HUMANITY
REALM OF   ASURA
SENSE-DESIRE   DEMON
ANIMAL
GHOST
HELLS—EIGHT LEVELS

Plate G. The Three Realms

centers around the great world-mountain Meru. The three realms as described comprise a Mount Meru world system.

B.   THE MOUNT MERU WORLD SYSTEM

Meru, the great central mountain of the universe, is an ancient Indian
cosmological conception common to both Hindu and Buddhist schools,
and is the basic model for the lower realms of the board.

The Meru world system includes the great mountain at the center,
eighty thousand miles high and as many underground.[43] Seas and continents surround it, with subterranean realms beneath and mansions floating
above. (See Plates H and I.) What modern scientific cosmologists call the
earth is considered to be a continent floating in the seas south of the central mountain called Jambu Island.

The great mountain is square: Its four sides, clockwise from the north,
are made of emerald, crystal, lapis lazuli, and ruby.[44] Each side colors the
continent below with its characteristic tint of reflected light. Jambu Island,

36

to the south (square No. 17), takes its characteristic sky-blue tone from the blue lapis lazuli of Meru's southern wall.

Surrounding Meru are seven circular mountains made of gold, and between them seven lakes, the first of which surrounds the central mountain itself. These lakes, called Sītās, diminish in size. They are cool, clear, and sweet. Outside the seventh gold mountain lies the great outer sea of salt water. In it are four continents, each with two satellites in their characteristic shape, inhabited by human beings and animals (square Nos. 17–20). Our southern continent, Jambu ("rose apple") Island, is shaped like a chariot; its twin satellites have the same shape. They are called East and West Chowrie. Nāgas, great serpents with rich palaces, live in all the lakes and seas. The saltiness of the ocean outside is explained as pollution from the earth.[45]

Outside the salt sea is a circular iron wall, bringing the world's major mountains to the magic number of nine (including Mount Meru, the seven mountains, and the iron wall).

All the hells discussed in the texts relate to Jambu Island. Those referred to as "temporary" are located on the surface of the earth—on mountain, desert, or water—and are the result of particular individual or collective deeds (square No. 8). Below the earth is the court of Yama, Lord of the Dead (square No. 9). Beneath this are the eight hot hells (square Nos. 2–6), each with sixteen appendices, and beside them the cold hells (square No. 7), "arranged shaftlike beneath one another, but in such a way that the middle or fourth hell is widest, and the top and bottom hell(s) the narrowest."[46] The lowest hot hell, called Avīci, "interminable" —for its sufferings have no intermission—is as far below sea level as is the peak of Meru above (square No. 2).

Yama is lord of the *pretas,* spirits who range underground and haunt places on earth such as cemeteries and caves. These include hungry ghosts (square No. 10) and other demons (square No. 14), many with supernatural powers. Asuras (square No. 15) are sometimes classed among them. They inhabit the lower slopes and interior of Meru and the chains of gold mountains. Above them are four classes of demigods, ruled by the kings of the cardinal directions (square No. 27). These reside on the peaks of the golden mountains, on Meru up to its summit, and on the planetary bodies. The four kings are "world protectors," looking over the realms below and forming a buffer between devas and asuras. Above them at Meru's summit are the palaces and parks of the Thirty-three Gods

Plate H. The Mount Meru World System

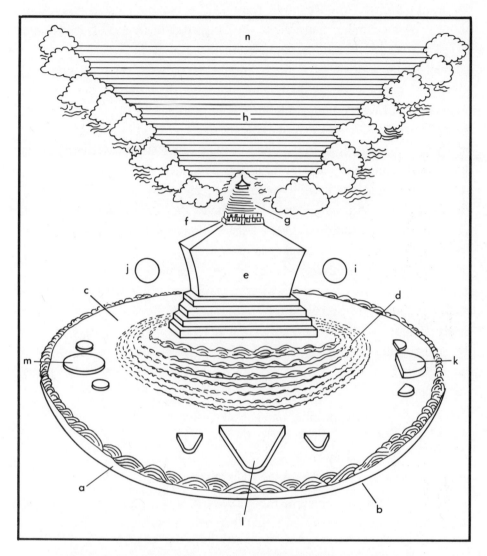

Plate I. Chart of the Mount Meru World System. (a) Iron Mountain; (b) Hungry Ghosts, Hot and Cold Hells; (c) Salt Seas; (d) Seven Lakes, Seven Mountains; (e) Mount Meru, South Side; (f) City of the Thirty-three Gods; (g) Indra's Palace; (h) High Devas, Form and Formless Gods; (i) Sun; (j) Moon; (k) Eastern Continent; (l) Jambu Island; (m) Western Continent (behind Mount Meru; Northern Continent); (n) Buddha Fields (square No. 28). Beyond these are the cloud mansions of the four higher classes of divinity of the Realm of Sense Desire (square Nos. 29–32), and above these the similar mansions of the Form Realm (square Nos. 35 and 37). The Formless Realm (square No. 36) has no "place."

Such is the scheme of a single Mount Meru world system, many of which comprise a larger world system, filling out the infinite expanse of the universe. The Meru system is elaborated in accord with the theory of karmic retribution, which is the root cause for one's position in sàmsāra.

Even the Form and Formless heavens are still a part of sàmsāra. Their divine inhabitants—or meditators at the equivalent level—although concentrated in mind, freed from sense desire, and subsisting on intellectual events are still subject to karma. Eventually the forces supporting their long life span are exhausted. Other karmic impulses then come into effect, and they enter an adjacent level or a lower destiny.

In the Buddhist analysis of religion, there are three trainings: morality, meditation, and study leading to wisdom. The first two, at least, are not exclusive properties of the Buddhist tradition. Only the wisdom of the true Dharma (based on the two others), an understanding of the nature of reality, leads to liberation from sàmsāra. Pure moral conduct, within or without the Dharma, tends to a deva rebirth. Meditational accomplishments without wisdom bring one to the state of the Form and Formless gods.

> By morality one gains heaven,
> by meditation the fortune of Brahma,
> By awareness of things as they are
> one comes to the state of nirvana.[47]

From the fifth row upward, the game is concerned primarily with the stages of the paths to liberation, rather than one's fortunes in the world.

C. THE RELIGIOUS TRADITIONS

The various spiritual paths are appropriate to the different types of human personality. In the system of Atīśa, there are three general types: (1) those who seek a happy rebirth, especially heaven, by the performance of good works; (2) those who seek liberation from sàmsāra; and (3) those whose goal is the emancipation of all beings.[48] All three are represented in the game as different religious traditions and as tendencies within Buddhism. To reach the highest levels of the board one must develop the attitude of the third type.

The various paths may be taken to represent the cultural diversity of humankind. In addition to the Buddhist paths there are barbarians, Hindus, and Bönists (square Nos. 21–23). These may also be interpreted as differing attitudes toward religion. Barbarism (square No. 21) stands for fanatical iconoclasm, materialism, and/or religious persecution. Hinduism (square No. 22) would represent the postulation of permanent principles: God and the soul. In medieval history, the Muslims in Asia were seen as barbarians who swept through Central Asia and across northern India attempting to dismember civilization. Thus, in iconography, the barbarians are represented as Turkish peoples.[49] Square No. 21 is the gateway to the Interminable, lowest of the hot hells and retribution for destruction of the Dharma. Nonetheless, it may also lead to mastery of the Hindu tradition, and this may be taken as acknowledgment that Muslims had the tendency to become civilized by the Indian environment, producing such fine hybrid flowerings as the Sufi and Sikh movements.

Bön (square No. 23) is most similar to Buddhism; it may be interpreted as the native shamanist legacy of any part of the world, grown more sophisticated in response to the missionary efforts of the supranational traditions. Both Bön in Tibet and Taoism in China developed their modern forms in reaction to Buddhism, as, similarly, the peyote cult in the Americas is a response to Christianity.

The four Buddhist vehicles represented are those of the Disciples and Independent Buddhas in rows five, six, and seven, and the Mahāyāna and its tantric alternative rising higher. The former are sometimes referred to as "inferior" (hīnayāna), in contrast to the Mahāyāna, "Greater Vehicle." This is somewhat misleading, because all the paths, as we have seen, are considered more or less appropriate for differing personality types at any given stage of their development.

In general, the Disciples and Independent Buddhas have goals that correspond to Atīśa's second way: seeking liberation for oneself alone (Disciples—square Nos. 38, 39, 40, and 51; Independent Buddhas—square Nos. 43–47). The Disciples are those who follow the teachings of the historical Buddha. Their major surviving sect (from an original eighteen) is referred to as "those following the doctrine of the elders" (in Sanskrit, *Sthaviravādin;* in Pāli, *Theravādin*). "Elders" refers to the senior monks and, possibly, nuns of the Buddhist community when it first divided into sects, from one to three centuries after the Buddha's parinirvana.

The goal of the Disciples is Arhatship (square No. 51), complete "capability" or, as the Buddhists understand the term, "conquering the enemy" —that is, gaining control over one's karmic destiny by annihilating the karmic defilements. One of the traps of the game is the tendency of the Disciples and Independent Buddhas to enter "Cessation" (square No. 48) —the state of nirvana resulting from victory over rebirth. The implication of this trap is that the practices of these lesser vehicles do not develop a commitment to the welfare of others. From the state of cessation it is very difficult to reawaken and resolve, as does the bodhisattva, to lead all beings to nirvana before escaping sàmsàra oneself. There is also a tendency in these preliminary vehicles to delude oneself and enter some heavenly existence that results from pure morality or meditative skill.

The Independent Buddhas attain a similar Arhatship (square No. 47) or fall into the same cessation. They differ from the Disciples in that they have not had the good fortune to be born during the time of a buddha. In their last life, at least, they have had to practice on their own and to come to their own understanding of the empty nature of the self. As a result, they do not formulate their insights in scriptural terms, the four noble truths, for example, but come to an independent understanding of karmic causality and the twelvefold chain of dependent origination. Because of their habits of solitude, and the lack of familiarity with formal teachings they find themselves unwilling and unable to teach others to any great extent—that is, to take on the tasks of the bodhisattva.

In brief, these two vehicles represent an aversion from existence, the Mahāyāna, the transcendence of this aversion.

Nonetheless, it is not considered appropriate to refer to the Disciples and Independent Buddhas as "inferior." The Tibetan masters acknowledge these two vehicles to be superior for that group of people who have the disposition and the good fortune to undertake them. The student of the Mahāyāna is taught that to denigrate the Vehicle of the Disciples to one who has no faith in the Greater Vehicle is to break his own bodhisattva vow by turning another being away from the Dharma.

In fact, all the vehicles are taught to be aspects of one another. The distinction made in the scriptures of highest meaning between the three types —disciple, independent Buddha, and bodhisattva—is said to be purely practical and without foundation in the ultimate truth. An example is that of the parent who returns home to find his house on fire. Standing in the street, he wonders how to save his three children, each on a different floor, for they are playful and immature, and there is not time to carry them out one by one. So he calls up to them from outside, "Hello, come out! I have some toys for you." And he promises to each his favorite toy—a deer-drawn cart, a goat cart, and a magnificent ox cart. When they arrive to find no toys at all, he points out that the house was burning around them, and in time imparts to each the very best ox-drawn cart.[50]

This parable illustrates the expedient means of the Buddha, the supremely competent teacher: The ultimate level of truth concerning the emptiness of reality may not be found in each of his doctrines, or may not be evident as such to each of his listeners. There is an intricate classification of the scriptures in terms of their levels of truth and their concealed or manifest nature. There is an overriding necessity, however, to escape the burning house of birth and death. The vehicles are individualized aspects of the single Great Vehicle of the Buddha's compassionate teachings that has as its aim the liberation of all.

The game board, however, is a concept based on the *relative* level of truth. Here the Lesser Vehicles, in order to rise any appreciable distance, must lead one to the beginning of the Mahāyāna (square No. 52). In what ways then is the Mahāyāna "greater," and why does only this path rise to the top of the board? Generally, because of the superiority in doctrine and in practice.

1. Whereas the Disciples and Independent Buddhas successfully overcome self-delusion, analyzing the psychophysical organism into its constituent elements (dharmas), in the Mahāyāna the elements themselves are shown to be fleeting, interdependent and ultimately without any stable and definable essence—empty.

2. Among the ways to liberation, the Mahāyāna places emphasis on the bodhisattva, who is committed by his vow to the salvation of all. This is the path leading to Buddhahood; it is known to the schools of the Disciples, but with time they have allowed its practice to lapse in favor of the more readily attainable state of Arhatship.

From the point of view of the bodhisattva

> There is no greater ingrate than one who,
> ignoring his destitute relatives bobbing up and down
> in the sea of birth and death,
> as though in a furious whirlpool,
> pursues his independent liberation.[51]

Without the attitude of the bodhisattva there would be no teaching and missionary activity, and so none of the Buddhist schools currently in existence can be said to properly represent the "Lesser Vehicle," for all attempt to teach and help others. It is hazardous to identify in more than a general way the Vehicles of the Disciples, as represented in this game, with that of the Theravādins of Śrī Laṅka (formerly called Ceylon). They represent only one of the eighteen ancient schools of the Lesser Vehicle. The Tibetans, furthermore, have had no acquaintance with any of the Theravādins in recent centuries. Sa-pan, who had some indirect knowledge of "Lesser Vehicle" monks from Śrī Laṅka and India, depicts the Vehicle of the Disciples as potentially leading to Buddhahood. In his day, monks of all the vehicles lived together in India, and it is obvious that they were virtually identical in lifestyle.[52] By the time of the modern version of Rebirth, if the educated Tibetan identified the "Lesser Vehicle" with any particular school, he would name the Sarvāstivāda and Sautrāntika, whose treatises are preserved in the Tibetan canon, and both of which are long defunct. The Disciples should be identified with a psychological attitude corresponding to Atīśa's second type of personality—one who holds inferior expectations of the path to liberation.

D. SIGNPOSTS ON THE ROAD TO AWAKENING

In an ancient conception common to all the vehicles, the way to liberation is divided into five "paths": Accumulation, Application, Vision, Meditative Cultivation, and Graduation. These paths are represented on the board in both the Vehicles of the Disciples (square Nos. 38–40 and 51) and the Independent Buddhas (square Nos. 43–47). The Path of Graduation or "no more study" is here synonymous with Arhatship (square Nos. 47 and 51).

The Mahāyāna consists of Sutra and Tantra vehicles. As these are the road to Buddhahood, the game board presents them in greater detail. Accumulation and Application are divided respectively into three and four grades (Sutra square Nos. 52–56 and 63–64; Tantra square Nos. 33, 41–42, 49–50, and 57–58). Beyond these two initial paths, however, is overlaid the later system of "bodhisattva stages." The Sutra Vehicle moves through these up the left side of the board, the Tantra up the right. Bodhisattva stages two through nine correspond to the Path of Cultivation, stage ten to Graduation. In this final stage, one is entitled a "bodhisattva great hero," and is one step removed from full Buddhahood.

The Tantra adds one lower stage (Beginning the Tantra, square No. 25) which is accessible not only to humans but to demons as well (the latter are forcibly converted). On the board, this is the lowest level at which one can enter a Buddhist path; it indicates the Tantra's consummate skill in means. The Sutra, on the other hand, is invariably entered by one abiding in Tushita Heaven (square No. 3), for this is the abode of the coming Buddha Maitreya, who is the source of many works expounding the sutras.

The course of practice of the Sutra division of the Mahāyāna does not differ radically, in its lower stages, from that of the lesser two vehicles. But it emphasizes the development of a more active compassion—making a commitment to the welfare of all fellow creatures—and its meditations culminate in the cognition of the ultimate emptiness of all phenomena. During his ten stages the bodhisattva develops into a world-saving hero, fulfilling the ideal of Atīśa's third personality type.

The Tantra division rides on the same two principles of compassion and emptiness, and so the game board shows this analogically by representing tantric progress through the same paths and stages.

Tantra is referred to as the Vehicle of Mantra. Magical patterns of syllables, called mantras, are fundamental tools in what may be termed the meditative manipulation and restructuring of reality. The goals of the tantra are the same as the Mahāyāna, but the practice is more intensive. Exercises in calm and insight, visualization and the contemplation of the emptiness of reality are practiced separately in the other vehicles, but are combined in the tantra in a single meditative ritual, thus turning the path into the goal. The tantra also elaborates yogic and symbolic techniques in an attempt to quickly and radically transmute the human body and emotions into the very vehicle of enlightenment. When successful, meditation leads the yogi to an actual experience of Buddhahood. Thus it is the quickest path, and the most dangerous. Tantric vows and regulations are extraordinarily severe. This path conceals the second "trap" of the board, Vajra Hell (square No. 1), reserved for those who break their tantric commitments. Also, descent may be made into the state of Rudra (square No. 16), the height of egotism and perversion of the doctrine, where those who use their magical accomplishments (siddhi) outside the constraints of morality and the bodhisattva vow reside. Yama (square No. 9) and Mahākāla (square No. 34) are possible stations on the tantric path, which represent the same wrathful energies, but liberated from egotism and bound to protection of the Dharma.

As in the Lesser Vehicles, meditation may result in the attainment of heavenly states of consciousness and/or control of material elements through visualization[53]; the tantric yogi may gain *siddhi* "accomplishment" and become a *vidyāhara* or wisdom-holder (row 9).

Vidyā simply means "knowledge," like "wisdom" (prajñā) in the feminine case. Wisdom-holders are Indian mythic figures from the oldest times —a phenomenal class of human beings who lived in the mountains and possessed magical powers, such as the ability to fly. This Tibetan historians take to indicate the secret existence of the tantras in ancient days.[54] In addition to the wisdom-holders of the Realm of Sense Desire (square No. 67), the game adds several others evolving from the Tantric Vehicle (square Nos. 68, 69, and 72). The masters of the Bön and Hindu traditions are also considered wisdom-holders equal in stature if less in potential, for they have reached the limit of development possible in their philosophic frameworks (square Nos. 62 and 65). The Buddhist wisdom-holders by contrast are bodhisattva yogis on the road to Buddhahood.

Connected with the two Mahāyāna roads are various mythic and world-transcending spheres. In the middle of the eighth row are three places thought to be situated on Earth: the Central Asian kingdom of Shambhala, the Potāla Mountain abode of the great-hero bodhisattvas Avalokiteśvara and Tārā, and Urgyan, land of the dakinis and birthplace of Padmasambhava. Among the squares of the three rows above these are Buddha fields. The Buddha field is a sphere purified by a Buddha in which the highest doctrines can be taught and easily put into practice without hindrance or distraction. It is said that Earth was a Buddha field while Śākyamuni was in the world,[55] but generally the fields are considered to fall outside the Meru world system, since they transcend sàmsāra.

The fields depicted in the game are those created by the five Buddha heads of the tantric "families" known in Tibet. Among them, only the "western paradise" of Amitābha and the "northern" of Akṣobhya seem to have been the object of widespread cult worship. Two others are obscure, and may have been invented by the Tibetans in order to complete the scheme. Upon rebirth the devotee resides in a Buddha field as a shortcut to enlightenment; the practice most appropriate to these distracted times. In the game (square Nos. 70, 76, 77, and 85), the players leap to these highest stages.

In the fifth Buddha field, the Supreme (Akaniṣṭha) Heaven (square No. 84), the tenth-stage bodhisattva takes final instruction from Buddha. Here the Buddha manifests his Enjoyment body with its miraculous characteristics not seen by ordinary creatures. From there, the bodhisattva attains the Dharma body (square No. 93), the unalloyed essence of the mystic Awakening. Then he or she in turn manifests the enjoyment body (square No. 92), and finally the emanation body (top row).[56] This latter should be pluralized, for, in fact, innumerable buddhas in as many world systems demonstrate the path to nirvana. The deeds of the Buddha in the realm of temporality, along the top row of the board, follow the pattern set by Śākyamuni in his sojourn on Earth. In the end, one enters nirvana (square No. 104).

* * *

The world view presented by this painting (board) is sophisticated and intricate, the product of centuries of development in India and Tibet. One could expound upon it far beyond the limits set by this introduction, for it contains, in essence, almost the whole of Buddhist thought. The present writer intends that the appended commentaries will provide sufficient material for the reader to follow the course of events in the game and come to his or her informed interpretation.[57]

⟨ VI ⟩

THE PAINTING

Pema Dorje, the artist who painted the board for this game, is a young Tibetan currently exiled in India. He lives in Manali, in the Himālayan foothills, and in a refugee camp in the state of Orissa. He is among the last generation of Tibetans able to systematize and create in exclusively traditional forms. The painting was done with traditional materials and with great care.

The Tibetan term for a cloth painting, tanka (thang-ka), implies a scroll.[58] The tanka is a picture—painted, embroidered, or appliquéd—that can be rolled up (from the bottom) for transport. In India and Tibet, it was traditionally a part of the paraphernalia of traveling teachers and storytellers. The Wheel of Life has been found painted on the cave walls of Ajanta, and is an enduring example of the type of paintings that illustrate teachings, as are biographical illustrations that derive from the forms found at the Indo-Greek school of Gandhāra, telling of the life of the Buddha. Modern Tibetan biographical paintings are highly stylized in form, giving the central figure's lineage and inspiring figures above, scenes of his life clockwise around the borders, and disciples, worshipers, and patrons below.

Tankas are also hung over shrines for purposes of worship, and used by yogis to help form their meditative visualization. In this tantric realm the painting (though nearly always rectangular) has the composition of a mandala, with the central figure placed in its field. The mandala itself, as used for initiations, is more often painted on the ground with colored sand; thus the most beautiful of Tibetan artwork becomes an example of the law of impermanence.

The painting of the game board is an illustration par excellence of Tucci's observation that "Tibetan painting . . . puts before us the symbols of spiritual planes."[59] Across the top are symbols of the exalted realms with which Tibetans most readily identify, Buddhas in temporal manifestation. To the left is Amitābha, "boundless light," the lord of the Western Continent called "land of bliss" (square No. 77). In the center is a stūpa, the final resting place of a buddha and depository of relics, either his physical remains after cremation or his legacy of sacred books. Stūpa is translated "support of worship" (mchod-rten, pronounced chörden) in Tibetan, for such is its function. It contains the relics of a fully Awakened personage. To the right is Padmasambhava, considered the second Buddha of our age, holding a vajra, skullcup, and trident. Each figure has its halo, dark blue with golden rays, and the stūpa is surrounded by a larger halo of flames. The two human figures have in addition a nimbus around the head. They are all three placed in the clouds, being extraterrestrial, and are situated in fields, indicated by mansion, pavilion, and garden. Such paintings of figures as these, as well as sculptured stūpas, are reputed to produce "liberation at sight" when perceived by a spiritually matured and purified imagination.

Paintings were created by workshops and schools within monastic walls or outside of them by families of lay craftsmen who were commissioned by monasteries or private patrons. Itinerant craftsmen would often visit different areas, painting in different styles and on any subject by request.

Painting is still considered one of the accomplishments of the well-educated monk.

The tanka usually has a linen surface, although silk is occasionally used. The material is stretched on a wooden frame with twine. Three rectangular sizes are specified in the Indian manuals but are rarely followed.[60] The cloth is spread with slaked lime mixed with animal glue or gum arabic, several times on each side, until it is well soaked. When the lime has hardened, it is burnished with a conch shell. The surface is thus rendered smooth and shiny, and with a background of lime white.

The outline is traditionally drawn with charcoal, but a lead pencil was used in this tanka. The iconographic size and outline are strictly determined by the prescriptions of the ritual texts, for otherwise the painting would be useless for worship and meditation. The iconometry of these paintings is a science; to stray from the proper forms would render the exercise baseless, as would astrology with mistakes in arithmetic or medicine without a proper diagnosis. The works on iconometry are specific in every detail.[61] Most painters are not expert in such forms; they are supplied by the monastic establishments with a sheaf of outlines printed from wood or metal blocks.

The lines as formed in space project the essence of things. The linear forms are manifestations of emptiness and are filled with symbol and color. The originality of the artist appears in noncanonical representations, or in details of form and color outside the central figures. In theory, the painter should re-create himself out of emptiness as well, being identified meditatively with the subject of the painting. In short, the painting should unfold in response to a true inner vision, in accord with the ritual meditations. The painter should ideally be saintly and learned; the studio should be prepared in the same manner as a meditation room.

Once the cloth is prepared, the outline is placed over it and punctured with a needle, which is then traced with charcoal, followed by red or black ink. Measurements are made exact by intersecting triangles, and the rectangles of the game board are formed in this way. This process is much the same as that used by Russian painters of icons and by Byzantine artists, and seems to have come west along with Mongolian conquests.

The outlines are filled with color, again in accordance with traditional prescriptions. Disciples will often do this, the master then finishing the work and adding the touches of gold to the halo or ornaments of the main figures. The colors are predominantly mineral, but some are vegetable. The major colors are lime white, red from cinnabar, yellow from arsenic or sulphur, green from vitriol, vermillion from carmine, and blue from lapis lazuli. They are ground in a mortar and mixed with lime, with gluten added to make them lasting. The brush has a bamboo or tamarisk handle and animal hairs bound with glue and silk thread.

The figure should be drawn on an auspicious day, especially the fifteenth of the lunar month, on the full moon. The eyes are colored last, this being accompanied by a special ceremony.

The completed tanka is sewn into a border made of strips of silk and brocade in red, yellow, and blue: rainbow colors, the light of the heavens and radiance of divinity. The colors should be chosen so as to lead the eye into the painting. A path of complementary color is sometimes sewn on the lower border. This is the "doorway" into the world of the tanka. At the bottom is a rolling stick with knobs of brass or silver. From the top hangs a veil of silk to protect the face of the painting from the smoky butter lamps placed before it on an altar, and two ribbons with which to tie it down in case of wind.[62]

The tanka must be enlivened by a ceremony of consecration. The main deity is evoked and its spirit drawn into the painting with a baptism of mantras, flowers, and water—the water being sprinkled onto a mirror image of the painting rather than directly on the cloth.[63]

*   *   *

The painting for this game was done in 1971 when the artist, a married layman, was twenty-four years of age. The original tanka is 18½ inches wide by 19¼ inches long. In conception and execution it is a *tour de force,* a marvel of skill in painting, knowledge of tradition, and Tibetan ingenuity.

The name of each state of rebirth is printed in capital letters in the middle or bottom of each square, along with a characteristic picture or symbol. The six letters inscribed on the Tibetan die are printed around the edges, reading left to right:

ས་　ཨ་　ག་　ད་　ར་　ཡ་

SA   A   GA   DA   RA   YA

Next to each of the letters is written, in cursive script, the name of the square to which that cast of the die corresponds. In the instructions below, the six letters are given as Arabic numerals ("one" and "two" being the first and best tosses), so that a Western die may be used.

The game was obtained by John Weir Hardy, a resident of India, and was brought to North America by Jody Kent, who has put great enlightened efforts into its presentation. A number of spelling mistakes may be noted,[64] as well as two errors of substance.[65]

·₀⟨ *Notes to the Introduction* ⟩₀·

1. An eyewitness reports that every third Chinese soldier carried a rifle, and the rest were armed with shovels. One should mention also the British expedition of 1904 (see Peter Fleming, *Bayonets to Lhasa* [New York: Harper & Row, 1961]). But the British had little cultural influence in Tibet. In fact, it was quite surprising to the Tibetans that the British, after all the time and expense involved in forcing the Lhasa government to capitulate, demanded essentially nothing more than to open a diplomatic mission and a trading post. The Chinese by contrast maintained a large garrison, which caused rampant inflation of food prices and was a great hardship on the general population. Comparing the two, the people of Lhasa said: "When you have to deal with a scorpion, the frog seems divine."

The best introduction to Tibet is R. A. Stein, *Tibetan Civilization,* trans. J. E. Stapleton Driver (Stanford, Calif.: Stanford University Press, 1972). See also David Snellgrove and Hugh Richardson, *A Cultural History of Tibet* (New York: Praeger Publishers, 1968).

2. See Mircea Eliade, *Shamanism: Archaic Techniques of Ecstasy,* Bollingen Series LXXVI (New York: Pantheon, 1964), esp. pp. 428–41, and the commentary and notes to square Nos. 23 and 65 below.

3. Tsepon W. D. Shakabpa, *Tibet: a Political History* (New Haven, Conn.: Yale University Press, 1967), pp. 26–36; Paul Demiéville, *Le Concile du Lhasa,* Bibliothèque de l'Institute des Hautes études Chinoises, Vol. 7 (Paris: Impr. Nat., 1952), esp. pp. 167ff.

4. On the debate see Demiéville, ibid.; G. Tucci, *Minor Buddhist Texts* II, Serie Oriental Roma, Vol. 9 (Rome: Instituto Italiano per il Medio ed Estremo Oriente [abbreviated SOR ISMEO], 1958); Bu-ston, *History of Buddhism,* trans. E. Obermiller, Bu-ston's *History of Buddhism* (Heidelberg: Otto Harrassowitz, 1931, 1932), reprinted Suzuki Research Foundation, Reprint Series

5 (Tokyo), pp. 191–96. The lineage of the Ch'an master, called simply Mahāyāna, whom the Tibetan King commanded from Tun Huang to defend the Chinese side, has not been determined. The master may have been either Northern or Southern Ch'an. The distinction may not in fact have existed in his Central Asian homeland, which was at that time ruled by the Tibetans and cut off from the Ch'an schools of T'ang China. The rivalry of the various Ch'an schools under the Chinese empire seems, to the non-Sinologist, to have been based more on competition for the limited scope and resources allowed Buddhism by the imperial court than on any significant doctrinal or practical divergences—whether meditation is done sitting, or all the time. The fruits of triumph fell to Shen-hui, upholder of the Southern School, not from his piety or religious accomplishment, but by pleasing the Emperor with his success in the sale of monk certificates during a time of financial crisis. To the Tibetans the differences between the Ch'an schools would have made no difference. For them Ch'an represented quietism. Whereas in China the Ch'an emphasis on meditation represented a genuine reaction to the overscholasticism and political involvements of its rival schools, in Tibet no such situation had been obtained, for the process of translation and scholastic investigation had barely begun. The view of the Chinese party that the root of sàmsāra is conceptualizing mind, and that the attainment, through meditation, of a state of mind unagitated by imaginings constitutes liberation is not in disaccord with the Indian Mahāyāna. But the monk Mahāyāna is pictured in Tibetan histories and in the dance dramatizations of the introduction of Buddhism as a clown who kicks away sacred texts that are cited against him, and teaches that sleep or unconsciousness is the most important thing, precisely because his rejection of intellectual activities, of study and moral practice, was not suited to the Tibetan environment of that time. Likewise, in China, when scholasticism was later destroyed by imperial persecution and most of Ch'an rivals had disappeared, Ch'an masters became the repository of all Buddhist teachings and techniques, and the Ch'an-Zen traditions have probably produced more literature than the other schools combined. (See Mark Tatz, "T'ang Influence During the Early Spread of Buddhism in Tibet," Vancouver, 1975, (unpublished examination paper, Department of Religious Studies, University of British Columbia), pp. 20ff.

5. Li An-che, "The Bka'-brgyud Sect of Lamaism," *Journal of the American Oriental Society,* LXIX 1949, p. 51.

6. A translation of this work, verses and autocommentary, has been done in the form of a Ph.D. dissertation by Fr. R. F. Sherburne, Asian Languages, University of Washington, Seattle.

7. *Biography of Dharmasvāmin,* trans. G. N. Roerich (Patna: K. P. Jayaswal Research Institute, 1958).

8. On Sa-pan and Sakya history see his *A Treasury of Aphoristic Jewels,* trans. James Bosson (University of Indiana, 1969), pp. 2–7 (from Mongol

sources); G. Tucci, *Tibetan Painted Scrolls,* (abbrev. TPS) (Libreria dello Stato, Rome, 1949), pp. 7–17 (in which the "Letter to the Tibetans" is translated in full); Shakabpa, op. cit., pp. 61ff.; Stein, op. cit., p. 163. Sa-pan's account of his defeat of the Hindus in *Sa-skya-pa'i Bka'-'bum,* V. Toyo Bunko (Tokyo, 1968), Vol. V., work 80. On Pag-pa see Tashi T. Densapa, *"Gro-mgon Chos-rgyal 'phags-pa, Blo-gros Rgyal-mtshan* (University of Washington, 1972, unpublished M.A. thesis).

9. Garma C. C. Chang, trans., *The Hundred Thousand Songs of Milarepa,* New York: University Books, 1962 (abbreviated *Milarepa*): Rolf Stein, *Vie et chants de 'Brug-pa kun-legs le yogin,* Paris, 1972; John Ardussi, *'Brug-pa kun-legs, the saintly Tibetan madman,* Seattle, Wash.: University of Washington, 1972 (unpublished M.A. thesis).

10. Courtesy of the current Bdag-chen Rinpoche of the Sakya royal family. Sa-pan is named as inventor of the game by lamas of the Sakya tradition, and this is borne out by the note of Sarat Chandra Das, *Journey to Lhasa and Central Tibet,* Royal Geographic Society, ed. W. W. Rockhill, (London: Murray, 1902), p. 260.

11. On the five arrows of Mañjuśrī see Alex Wayman, *The Buddhist Tantras* (New York: Samuel Weiser, Inc., 1973), Ch. 15.

12. *Snyigs-ma, kaṣāya,* "defiled" or full of "foul substance." On the five types of neurosis, see *Mahāvyutpatti* (abbrev. MHV), ed. Sakaki Ryōzaburō (Kyoto, 1916), repr. Suzuki Research Foundation, Nos. 2335ff.

13. T. Norbu, *Tibet Is My Country,* as told to Heinrich Harrer, tr. E. Fitzgerald (London: Hart-Davis, 1960), p. 93.

14. Stewart Culin in *Report of the National Museum* (Washington, D.C.: Smithsonian Institution, 1893), pp. 504–7; 1896, pp. 820–21. Thanks for these and the next three references to John W. Hughes of the University of Washington, an enviably meticulous scholar.

15. Ibid., 1893, p. 503.

16. Stewart Culin, *Games of the Orient* (Philadelphia: University of Pennsylvania Press, 1895), p. 76.

17. Quoted by H. J. R. Murray, *A History of Chess* (Oxford: Clarendon Press, 1913), p. 34.

18. Harish Johari, *Leela* (New York: Coward, McCann and Geoghegan, Inc., 1975), Nos. 61, 13.

19. Culin, *Games,* p. xviii.

20. L. Augustine Waddell, *The Buddhism of Tibet, or Lamaism* (Cambridge, Mass.: W. Heffer and Sons, 1939), pp. 471–73. The game reproduced here, possibly truncated, has fifty-six squares. The author views it as a device of the lamas to extract money from relatives of the deceased. There is no board for this purpose, although divination boards do exist for the more immediate deci-

sions of this life (see Emil Schlagentweit, *Buddhism in Tibet,* repr. Susil Gupta [London, 1968], Ch. XVII). Since the time of Waddell, the "crossing the bardo" text, known to the West as *The Tibetan Book of the Dead,* has been discovered, which contains the rituals and instructions relevant to the deceased. Sarat Chandra Das correctly identified Rebirth as a game in 1904; loc. cit. note 9 above.

21. *Majjhima-nikāya,* after the translation of I. B. Horner, *The Middle Length Sayings* Vol. I, Pali Text Society (abbrev. PTS) Translation Series No. 29 (London: Luzac and Co., 1954), pp. 10–11.

22. *Dīgha-nikāya,* ed. T. W. Rhys Davids and J. E. Carpenter, Pali Text Society (London: Luzac and Co., 1890, repr. 1967), pp. 12–17; tr. also T. W. Rhys Davids, *Dialogues of the Buddha* (London: Henry Frowde, 1899), pp. 16–30. See also *Book of the Kindred Sayings* (Samyutta-nikāya), tr. F. L. Woodward, Vol. III, Pali Text Society Translation Series No. 13 (London: Luzac and Co., 1954), pp. 190–91.

23. Edited in Sanskrit by Raghu Vira and Lokesh Candra, *Kālacakra Tantra and Other Texts,* Parts 1 and 2 (New Delhi: International Academy of Indian Culture, 1966). See references in notes to Square No. 59 below; also Csoma de Koros, "On the Origins of the Kālacakra System," *Journal of the Asiatic Society of Bengal* (abbrev. JASB) II, 57; *A Grammer of the Tibetan Languages in English* (Calcutta, 1834, repr. Altai Press, Triad Reprints), p. 192.

24. *Tohoku Catalogue of the Tibetan Buddhist Canon* (Sendai, 1934), No. 4322. See the commentary of Pad-dkar Yid-bzhin dbang-po, *Dbyangs-'char 'grel-pa,* ed. with an Introduction in English by Sonam Kazi (Gangtok, 1970).

25. See commentary to Square No. 59 below.

26. On military magic see Sonam Kazi, ed. and Introduction, *Encylopedia Tibetica: The Collected Works of Bo-dong pan-chen Phyogs-las rnam-rgyal,* (New Delhi: Tibet House), Vols. 2 and 5.

27. On divination boards see references to note 20 above, and the same sources on other means of divination. Waddell's is still the best account of astrology. On these subjects see the chapters of Réne de Nebesky-Wojkowitz, *Oracles and Demons of Tibet* (The Hague: Mouton and Co., 1956); David Snellgrove, *The Nine Ways of Bön* (London: Oxford University Press, 1967) (see especially the first "way"); and Sir Charles Bell, *The People of Tibet* (Oxford: Clarendon Press, 1928). On divination by lightning see J. Bacot, "La Table de Présages signifiés par l'éclair," *Journal Asiatique* (abbrev. JA) (1913), pp. 445–49. On divination from birds see B. Laufer, "Bird Divination Among the Tibetans," *T'oung Pao* (abbrev. TP) 15 (1914), pp. 1–100. Nebesky-Wojkowitz (above) provides other refs., p. 455n.

28. *Sa-gnon rnam-bzhags.* Since the inventor was a pandit, we may

presume to re-create the Sanskrit title: *bhūmyākramaṇa-vyavasthāpana.* The Bhutanese game is known as "Determination of the Paths to the Stages" (sa lam rnam-bzhags), for its goal is to reach the flight of bodhisattva stages at the top of the board.

29. See for example Alfonsa Ferrai, *mK'yen-brtse's Guide to the Holy Places of Central Tibet,* completed L. Petech and H. L. Richardson, SOR Vol. 16 (Rome: ISMEO, 1958); and T. V. Wylie's editions and translations of sections of the *'Dzam-gling rgyas-bshad,* "Extensive Explanation of Jambu Island," of Bla-ma Btsan-po: *The Geography of Tibet,* SOR Vol. 15 (Rome: ISMEO, 1962); *A Tibetan Religious Geography of Nepal,* SOR (Rome: ISMEO, 1970).

30. On dependent origination see Lama Anagarika Govinda, *Foundations of Tibetan Mysticism* (London: Rider and Co., 1959), pp. 241–47; A. Foucher, *The Life of the Buddha,* abridged tr. Simone Brangier Boas (Middletown, Conn.: Wesleyan University Press, 1936), pp. 117–19.

31. The preceding two paragraphs are paraphrased from His Holiness Tenzin Gyatsho, the XIVth Dalai Lama, *The Opening of the Wisdom Eye* (Bangkok: Social Science Association Press of Thailand, 1968), pp. 18–22.

32. Buddhist *karma,* "activity," is distinct from *karma,* "social obligation" of the theistic Hindu schools, such as that of the *Bhagavad Gītā.*

33. From "The Stanzas of Dhārmika Subhūti," ed. Paul Mus, *La Lumière sur les Six Vois* (Paris: Université de Paris Travaux et Mémoires de l'Institut d'Ethnologie XXXV, 1939), pp. 216–17.

34. Paul Mus, ibid.; "The Scripture on Mindfulness of the True Doctrine" (saddharma-smrti-upasthāna-sūtra), studied in part by Lin Li-Kouang, *L'Aide-mémoire de la Vraie Loi, Dharma-samuccaya, Compendium de la Loi,* Vol. I Publications de Musée Guimet, Bibliothèque d'Études Vol. 53 (Paris: Adrien Maisonneuve, 1946), and by Daigan and Alicia Matsunaga, *The Buddhist Concept of Hell* (New York: Philosophical Library, 1972); also, *L'Abhidharmakośa de Vasubandhu* (abbrev. AK), tr. Louis de La Vallée Poussin, Société Belge d'Études Orientales (Paris: Paul Geuthner, 1923–1931), esp. Chs. III–IV.

35. Lin, op. cit., pp. 63–64.

36. Ibid. pp. 68ff.; Govinda, op. cit., chart p. 253 and discussion pp. 250ff.

37. Śāntideva, *Bodhicaryāvatāra,* Chapter V, verses, 1–3, Sanskrit and Tibetan ed. V. Bhattacharya, Bibliotheca Indica (Calcutta: The Asiatic Society, 1960).

38. Lin, op. cit., pp. 246ff.

39. A. K. Warder, *Indian Buddhism* (Delhi: Motilal Banarsidass, 1970), p. 127. On seven stations of consciousness, of which this is the first, see also AK, III. 16ff.

40. In Sa-pan's game the Form and Formless Realms are not named as such—it has instead the eight trances and equalizations, plus a square called "Long-lived Gods."

41. On Brahmā, see Warder, op. cit., pp. 143–44; AK, III. 17, VIII. 180–82; Étienne Lamotte, *Histoire du Bouddhisme Indien,* Bibliothèque du Muséon, Vol. 43 (Louvan, 1958), p. 761. Buddhist literature does not seem to know the neuter *brahman,* the Absolute of the Vedāntins. This masculine *brahmā* is not, however, the Vedic god from among the Thirty-three; it seems to correspond to the Absolute of the Hindu schools, ignoring the change of gender that would ruin a good story.

42. In Sa-pan's game the Buddha fields are classed with the deva realms and so this anomaly would not occur, although the Akaniṣṭha is not represented there as such.

43. The unit of measure is the *yojana,* but this has a value that fluctuates between four and sixteen miles, according to the text. See W. M. McGovern, *A Manual of Buddhist Philosophy* (New York: E. P. Dutton & Co., 1923), pp. 42–43. On the Meru system see ibid., Part I; AK, Ch. III; R. Spence Hardy, *A Manual of Buddhism* (London: Partridge and Oakey, 1853), Ch. I (from Pāli sources); *The Lamp of Certainty by 'Jam-mgon Kong-sprul,* tr. Judith Hanson, University of British Columbia, (unpublished M.A. thesis), Vancouver, pp. 135–40. In the following discussion, details such as size and distances, length of ages, and life spans have been kept to a minimum; they are not relevant to the game and may be found in McGovern, Hardy, and the AK.

44. This follows the later Tibetan system; see Hanson, loc. cit. The AK gives gold, silver, lapis, and crystal (III. 142); the Pāli (from Hardy, p. 11), gold, silver, sapphire, and coral.

45. Three explanations are given for the saltiness of this ocean: pollution from a great fish, the magic of an evil rishi of old, and the earth's impurities being washed into the sea (McGovern, op. cit., p. 54).

46. Ibid., p. 62; see also AK, III. 148ff., on the hells.

47. Mus, op. cit., p. 288, n. 101; this translation done from the Pāli version.

48. Atīsa, *Lam-sgron,* v. 38. See also Tsong-kha-pa, *Lam-rim chung-ba,* Lhasa blockprint p. 66; Bu-ston, op. cit., I, pp. 81ff. There are earlier theories of three personalities, e.g., AK, VI. 199; Asaṅga, *Mahāyāna-sūtrālaṁkāra, Exposé de la doctrine du grand véhicule* (abbrev. MSA), tr. Sylvain Lévi, (Paris: Bibliothèque de l'Ecole des Hautes Études, fasc. 190, Librairie Honoré Champion, 1911), V, 5.

49. See, for example, Chögyam Trungpa, *Visual Dharma* (Berkeley, Calif.: Shambhala, 1975), Pl. 18.

50. *Lotus Sūtra,* Ch. III. See the translation of H. Kern, *Saddharma-puṇ-ḍarīka, or The Lotus of the True Law,* Sacred Books of the East (abbrev. SBE) XXI (Oxford: Clarendon Press, 1884), pp. 72ff.

51. Candragomin, *Śiṣyalekha,* v. 95, Sanskrit, ed. I. P. Minayeff (Leningrad: Russkoe Archaeologicheskoe Obshchestvo). *Vostochnoe Otdielenie, Zapiski,* Vol. 4, p. 51 (1889). Cf. Tibetan and tr. G. N. Roerich, *The Blue Annals* (abbrev. BA) (Calcutta: Royal Asiatic Society of Bengal, 1949, 1953), p. 840.

52. Dharmasvāmin, op. cit., pp. 73–74, records some antipathy from the disciples at Bodhgaya regarding the texts of the Mahāyāna. Yet he reports he found them more hospitable in general than monks of the Greater Vehicle whom he visited elsewhere (op. cit., p. 87).

53. For example, Buddhaghosa, *Visuddhimagga,* tr. Bhikkhu Ñyānamoli as *The Path of Purification* (Colombo: A. Semage, 1964), p. 182: "The fire kasina is the basis for such powers as smoking, flaming, causing showers of sparks, countering fire with fire, ability to burn only what one wants to burn, causing light for the purpose of seeing visible objects with the divine eye, burning up the body by means of the fire element at the time of attaining nibbana."

54. See references in notes to Square No. 67.

55. *Vimalakīrti-nirdeśa-sūtra,* tr. Étienne Lamotte as *L'Enseignement de Vimalakīrti,* Bibliothèque du Muséon Vol. 51 (Louvain: Publications Universitaires, 1962), pp. 120–21.

56. The three bodies are pictured in W. Y. Evans-Wentz, *The Tibetan Book of the Great Liberation* (London: Oxford University Press, 1954), p. 192.

57. Sources for the commentary are indicated in the annotation. I have relied as much as possible on the scriptures and treatises translated into Tibetan and used by native scholars during the Later Spread of the Dharma. The basic texts are common to other Buddhist traditions, but I have supplemented the commentaries only sparingly from Pāli and Chinese materials. For cosmology the basic texts are the "Scripture on Mindfulness" as studied by Lin and Matsunaga (op. cit., n. 34 above), the most sophisticated work of its kind, translated into Tibetan in the tenth to eleventh centuries, and the older texts studied by Paul Mus (n. 31). The *Abhidharmakośa* (n. 34) is of course for the Tibetans the authoritative treatise on psychology and the world. The spiritual paths and stages are interpreted according to the same sources used by Gampopa in his *Rnam-par thar-ba'i rgyan* (twelfth century, tr. H. V. Guenther as *The Jewel Ornament of Liberation,* repr. Clear Light Series [Berkeley, Calif.: Shambhala, 1971]). The tantras are systematized according to the Gelugpa scholar Mkhas-grub-rje (fifteenth century, *Fundamentals of the Buddhist Tantras,* tr. F. D. Lessing and Alex Waymen [The Hague: Mouton, 1968]), al-

though present-day systems differ in emphasis. For reasons of time and convenience, and to demonstrate that adequate materials for the interpretation of Buddhism in all its major aspects are available in Western languages, I have for the most part avoided consulting works in the original, the major exceptions to this policy being the retranslation of quoted passages to my own standards and taste. On several points, however, I have had the benefit of advice from, among others, the venerable Dezhung Rinpoche, learned lama of the Sakya sect, and from the young but skilled lama Trinlay Drubpa ('Phrin-las grub-pa), a Karma Kagyu from Bhutan. It is not possible to write a commentary of this sort, selecting from various sources, without in effect forming a system of one's own. The overriding consideration has been to explicate the painter's intentions as revealed in the game board, but the final responsibility for interpretation rests with me alone.

58. *Thang-ka* is not a literal translation of the Sanskrit *paṭa,* which simply means "cloth" and is applied to paintings and banners. "Cloth painting" would be in Tibetan *ras-bris* or *ras ri-mo.* So the nuances of the term must be sought in the Tibetan language. *Thang-ka* is a term of the Later Spread. Trungpa derives it from "thang yig . . . 'written record' "; *thang-ka* would thus indicate a "[visual] record" (*Visual Dharma,* p. 16). But *yig* is the part of the compound indicating "record"; *thang-yig* means "record of the realm." *Thang* would indicate "record" only as part of a compound—e.g., *bka'-thang,* "sovereign record," as short for *bka'i thang-yig,* "sovereign records of the realm." There is no indication that *thang-ka* is short for *thang-yig-ka,* which would be poor-sounding Tibetan indeed. *Thang* by itself indicates a "plain," so *thang-ka* would on the face of it indicate "something flat" or "vast." But it may in another way derive from *thang-yig.* This last is part of a set of terms indicating the oldest Tibetan writings (A.D. 655), royal commands and written codes of law: *bka' khrims,* "sovereign laws," and *thang-khrims gyi yi-ge,* "records of law for the realm" (Stein, op. cit., p. 59; Bacot et al., *Documents de Touen-Housang* [Paris: 1940–46]; F. W. Thomas, *Tibetan Literary Texts and Documents Concerning Chinese Turkestan,* Vol. I [London: 1935], p. 270, n. 2, p. 287, and n. 3). These were handwritten scrolls. So like the English word "volume," from *volumen,* "roll," there is *thang-ka* from *thang-yig,* meaning "scroll" (cf. TPS, p. 267).

59. TPS, p. 287.

60. Ibid., p. 267.

61. The texts reviewed ibid., pp. 291–99.

62. This account from George Roerich, *Tibetan Paintings,* Librairie Orientaliste (Paris: Paul Guethner, 1925), pp. 16–20; TPS, pp. 267–71, 286–308; C. Trungpa, op. cit., pp. 16–17.

63. TPS, pp. 308–16.

64. Just for the record, minor emendations:

Nos. 1 and 48: The number of letters to be thrown increases clockwise around the square. Translating this literally into our numbering system, one would have "After throwing 'one' once, 'two' twice, 'four' thrice, 'six' four times, 'five' five times, and 'three' six times, move to . . ."

Nos. 22 and 62: Read *mu-stegs* for *mu-rtegs*.

No. 23: Read *bon-po* for *bon-bo*.

No. 29: Read *'thab* for *thab*.

Nos. 41 and 53: Read *'bring* for *'breng*.

No. 44: "Three" should go to No. 45, not No. 43.

No. 45: "Three" should go to No. 46, not No. 43.

Nos. 49 and 55: Read *drod* for *grod*.

No. 59: Read *Sham-bha-la* for *Sham-bha-lha*.

No. 60: Read *Po-tā-la* for *Po-ṭa-la'o*.

No. 76: Read *brtsegs* for *rtsegs*. "Five" should move to Second Tantra, not Fifth; likewise for other numberings in this series.

No. 97: Read *bsdams-pa* for *stams-ba*.

No. 103: Read *bstan-pa* for *rtan-pa*.

65. Emendations of substance:

1. The shapes as painted of the Eastern and Western Continents (Nos. 18–19) should be reversed.

2. At No. 33 insert "Throwing 'five,' go to Rudra (No. 16)."

Rules of Play

Any number can play. The start is Square No. 24, "The Heavenly Highway." Each player places some token on this square. The low roll of the die moves first.

Throwing the die, the first player moves to the designated square. For example, a "two" moves to Jambu Island (square No. 17 on the board). Then the die is passed clockwise to the next player. If this player casts "four," he is born an animal (square No. 11), and passes the die again to the left. On his next move, Player 1 throws a "two" again, starting the tantric path (square No. 25), and so forth.

Ten "two"s in a row take one to Dharma body (square No. 93) and full Buddhahood via the tantric path. Ten "one"s from the beginning take one to the same place by way of the Mahāyāna. In a number of squares not all six numbers cause a move. The player throwing one of these "dead" numbers stays there another turn.

Two of the squares, Cessation in the Vehicle of the Disciples (square No. 48) and Vajra Hell (square No. 1), are traps. Here one must throw "one" once, "two" twice, "three" three times, and so forth through all six numbers. However, one may keep throwing in the same turn until a number comes up that one does not need. So the player in such a trap should check off the numbers needed as they are thrown, and stop throwing only when he gets one he doesn't need. If, for example, he starts off by throwing two "one"s in a row, he quits after the second and waits until his next turn. Throwing "one" again, he must pass to the next player.

The winner is the first to reach nirvana (square No. 104). From there your token is passed to the stūpa above and becomes the object of reverence and devotion.

//Sarva-maṅgalaṁ—Good Luck to All//

97 ADOPTING A PHYSICAL FORM	98 THE SETTING FORTH	99 ASCETIC PRACTICES	100 CONQUEST OF MĀRA	101 BUDDHAHOOD	102 TURNING THE WHEEL OF DHARMA	103 DEMONSTRATION OF MIRACLES	104 NIRVANA
ONE → OR → 98	ONE → OR → 99	ONE → OR → 100	ONE → OR → 101	ONE → OR → 102	ONE → OR → 103	ONE → OR → 104	ONE OR TWO → PASS YOUR RELICS INTO THE STUPA ABOVE AND BECOME AN OBJECT OF REVERENCE FOR THE REST OF THE AGE.
TWO	TWO	TWO	TWO	TWO	TWO	TWO	

89 EIGHTH TANTRA STAGE	90 NINTH TANTRA STAGE	91 TENTH TANTRA STAGE	92 GREAT ENJOYMENT BODY	93 GREAT DHARMA BODY	94 TENTH SUTRA STAGE	95 NINTH SUTRA STAGE	96 EIGHTH SUTRA STAGE
ONE → 84	ONE → 84	ONE → 84	ONE → 97	ONE → 92	ONE → 93	ONE → 94	ONE → 94
TWO → 90	TWO → 91	TWO → 93			TWO → 84	TWO → 84	TWO → 95

81 FIFTH TANTRA STAGE	82 SIXTH TANTRA STAGE	83 SEVENTH TANTRA STAGE	84 SUPREME HEAVEN	85 REALM OF SUPERJOY	86 SEVENTH SUTRA STAGE	87 SIXTH SUTRA STAGE	88 FIFTH SUTRA STAGE
ONE → 83	ONE → 89	ONE → 84	ONE → 93	ONE → 71	ONE → 95	ONE → 96	ONE → 95
TWO → 89	TWO → 90	TWO → 91		TWO → 73	TWO → 96	TWO → 86	TWO → 87
				THREE → 76			

73 SECOND TANTRA STAGE	74 THIRD TANTRA STAGE	75 FOURTH TANTRA STAGE	76 REALM OF JEWELED PEAKS	77 LAND OF BLISS	78 FOURTH SUTRA STAGE	79 THIRD SUTRA STAGE	80 SECOND SUTRA STAGE
ONE → 75	ONE → 75	ONE → 82	ONE → 78	ONE → 71	ONE → 87	ONE → 88	ONE → 78
TWO → 81	TWO → 81	TWO → 83	TWO → 74	TWO → 74	TWO → 88	TWO → 78	TWO → 79
SIX → 69		THREE → 81	THREE → 73				

65 WISDOM-HOLDER OF THE BÖN TRADITION	66 FIRST TANTRA STAGE	67 WISDOM-HOLDER AMONG THE GODS OF SENSE-DESIRE	68 WISDOM-HOLDER OF THE REALM OF FORM	69 TANTRIC WHEEL-TURNING KING	70 REALM OF ACTION-COMPLETION	71 FIRST SUTRA STAGE	72 WISDOM-HOLDER OF THE EIGHT SIDDHIS
ONE → 52	ONE → 74	ONE → 41	ONE → 42	ONE → 75	ONE → 86	ONE → 79	ONE → 67
TWO → 43	TWO → 75	TWO → 42	TWO → 49	TWO → 81	TWO → 73	TWO → 80	TWO → 41
FIVE → 15	THREE → 73	THREE → 68	FOUR → 59		FOUR → 34	THREE → 74	THREE → 33
SIX → 8		FOUR → 69	SIX → 41		FIVE → 74		
					SIX → 71		

57 TANTRA, PATH OF APPLICATION: "RECEPTIVITY"	58 TANTRA, PATH OF APPLICATION: "HIGHEST TEACHINGS"	59 SHAMBHALA	60 POTĀLA	61 URGYAN	62 HINDU WISDOM-HOLDER	63 MAHĀYĀNA, PATH OF APPLICATION: "RECEPTIVITY"	64 MAHĀYĀNA, PATH OF APPLICATION: "HIGHEST TEACHINGS"
ONE → 66	ONE → 73	ONE → 63	ONE → 64	ONE → 89	ONE → 52	ONE → 85	ONE → 71
TWO → 73	TWO → 74	TWO → 50	TWO → 63	TWO → 84	TWO → 38	TWO → 42	TWO → 49
THREE → 58	THREE → 66	THREE → 60	THREE → 42	THREE → 83		THREE → 64	FIVE → 77
FOUR → 77	FOUR → 85	FOUR → 49				FOUR → 77	
		FIVE → 42					
		SIX → 55					

Plate J. Translation and Moves for the Game of Rebirth

The Game of Liberation (board)

49 — TANTRA, PATH OF APPLICATION: "HEAT"
ONE → 50
TWO → 57

41 — TANTRA, MIDDLE PATH OF ACCUMULATION
ONE → 60
TWO → 42
THREE → 59
FIVE → 67
SIX → 33

33 — TANTRA, LESSER PATH OF ACCUMULATION
ONE → 41
TWO → 42
FIVE → 16
SIX → 1

25 — BEGINNING THE TANTRA
ONE → 72
TWO → 33
SIX → 38

17 — THE SOUTHERN CONTINENT
ONE → 52
TWO → 25
THREE → 26
FOUR → 22
FIVE → 16
SIX → 6

9 — LORD OF THE DEAD (YAMA)
ONE → 42
TWO → 34

1 — VAJRA HELL
ONE → ONCE
TWO → TWICE
THREE → 3 TIMES
FOUR → 4 TIMES
FIVE → 5 TIMES
SIX → 6 TIMES
GO TO 9.

---

50 — TANTRA, PATH OF APPLICATION: "CLIMAX"
ONE → 57
TWO → 66

42 — TANTRA, GREATER PATH OF ACCUMULATION
ONE → 49
TWO → 50
SIX → 59

34 — MAHĀKĀLA
ONE → 61
TWO → 81
THREE → 70

26 — WHEEL-TURNING KING
ONE → 29
TWO → 28
THREE → 17
FOUR → 13
FIVE → 13
SIX → 13

18 — THE WESTERN CONTINENT
ONE → 38
TWO → 27
THREE → 13
FOUR → 11
FIVE → 8
SIX → 4

10 — HUNGRY GHOSTS (PRETA)
ONE → 29
TWO → 28
THREE → 17
FOUR → 8
FIVE → 4

2 — INTERMINABLE HELL
ONE → 17
TWO → 10
THREE → 3

---

51 — DISCIPLES, ARHATSHIP
ONE → 52
TWO → 48
THREE → 37

43 — INDEPENDENT BUDDHA, PATH OF ACCUMULATION
ONE → 52
TWO → 44
THREE → 28
FOUR → 38
FIVE → 13
SIX → 6

35 — REALM OF FORM
ONE → 37
TWO → 52
THREE → 36
FOUR → 17
FIVE → 27
SIX → 27

27 — HEAVEN OF THE FOUR GREAT KINGS
ONE → 28
TWO → 17
THREE → 23
FOUR → 18
FIVE → 10
SIX → 6

19 — THE EASTERN CONTINENT
ONE → 43
TWO → 38
THREE → 13
FOUR → 13
FIVE → 11

11 — ANIMALS
ONE → 27
TWO → 17
THREE → 12
FOUR → 10
FIVE → 5

3 — THE HOT AND VERY HOT HELLS
ONE → 11
TWO → 10
THREE → 8
FOUR → 7
FIVE → 5
SIX → 2

---

52 — MAHĀYĀNA, LESSER PATH OF ACCUMULATION
ONE → 54
TWO → 53
THREE → 30
FOUR → 38
FIVE → 11
SIX → 7

44 — INDEPENDENT BUDDHA, PATH OF APPLICATION
ONE → 30
TWO → 46
THREE → 45
FOUR → 20
FIVE → 39
SIX → 27

36 — THE FORMLESS REALM
ONE → 38
TWO → 17
THREE → 11
SIX → 4

28 — HEAVEN OF THE THIRTY-THREE
ONE → 29
TWO → 17
THREE → 20
FOUR → 22
FIVE → 11
SIX → 7

20 — THE NORTHERN CONTINENT
ONE → 28
TWO → 27
THREE → 17
FOUR → 15
FIVE → 15

12 — DIVINE ANIMALS
ONE → 28
TWO → 27
THREE → 15
FOUR → 11
FIVE → 10

4 — THE HOWLING AND GREAT HOWLING HELLS
ONE → 13
TWO → 10
THREE → 8
FOUR → 6
FIVE → 3

---

53 — MAHĀYĀNA, MIDDLE PATH OF ACCUMULATION
ONE → 55
TWO → 54
THREE → 37
FOUR → 40
FIVE → 15
SIX → 8

45 — INDEPENDENT BUDDHA, PATH OF VISION
ONE → 52
TWO → 47
THREE → 46
FOUR → 40
FIVE → 17
SIX → 28

37 — PURE ABODES
ONE → 64
TWO → 54
THREE → 32
FOUR → 52
FIVE → 12

29 — HEAVEN WITHOUT FIGHTING
ONE → 30
TWO → 31
THREE → 17
FOUR → 23
FIVE → 12
SIX → 10

21 — BARBARISM
ONE → 15
TWO → 62
THREE → 13
FOUR → 11
FIVE → 10
SIX → 2

13 — WORLD OF THE NĀGAS
ONE → 28
TWO → 27
THREE → 15
FOUR → 11
FIVE → 10

5 — THE BLACK ROPE AND CRUSHING HELLS
ONE → 13
TWO → 10
THREE → 8
FOUR → 7
FIVE → 3

---

54 — MAHĀYĀNA, GREATER PATH OF ACCUMULATION
ONE → 63
TWO → 55
THREE → 60
FOUR → 59

46 — INDEPENDENT BUDDHA, PATH OF CULTIVATION
ONE → 30
TWO → 47
THREE → 37
FOUR → 35
FIVE → 51
SIX → 29

38 — DISCIPLES, PATH OF ACCUMULATION
ONE → 37
TWO → 40
THREE → 39
FOUR → 52
FIVE → 11
SIX → 5

30 — THE JOYFUL HEAVEN
ONE → 64
TWO → 63
THREE → 55
FOUR → 54
FIVE → 53
SIX → 52

22 — HINDUISM
ONE → 52
TWO → 65
THREE → 29
FOUR → 27
FIVE → 11
SIX → 3

14 — DEMON ISLAND
ONE → 25
TWO → 42
THREE → 17
FOUR → 15
FIVE → 5
SIX → 3

6 — REVIVING HELL
ONE → 17
TWO → 12
THREE → 10
FOUR → 8
FIVE → 5
SIX → 4

---

55 — MAHĀYĀNA, PATH OF APPLICATION "HEAT"
ONE → 63
TWO → 56

47 — INDEPENDENT BUDDHA, ARHATSHIP
ONE → 52
TWO → 48
THREE → 30
FOUR → 37

39 — DISCIPLES, PATH OF APPLICATION
ONE → 52
TWO → 43
THREE → 40
FOUR → 52
SIX → 19

31 — DELIGHTING IN EMANATIONS
ONE → 52
TWO → 30
THREE → 43
FOUR → 32
FIVE → 22
SIX → 12

23 — BÖN
ONE → 52
TWO → 30
THREE → 43
FOUR → 32
FIVE → 12
SIX → 44

15 — ASURAS
ONE → 28
TWO → 14
THREE → 21
FOUR → 11
FIVE → 10
SIX → 4

7 — THE COLD HELLS
ONE → 15
TWO → 18
THREE → 11
FOUR → 8
FIVE → 6
SIX → 5

---

56 — MAHĀYĀNA, PATH OF APPLICATION: "CLIMAX"
ONE → 64
TWO → 63

48 — CESSATION
ONE → ONCE
TWO → TWICE
THREE → 3 TIMES
FOUR → 4 TIMES
FIVE → 5 TIMES
SIX → 6 TIMES
GO TO 52.

40 — DISCIPLES, PATHS OF VISION AND CULTIVATION
ONE → 30
TWO → 35
THREE → 28
FOUR → 32
FIVE → 31
SIX → 29

32 — RULING THE EMANATIONS OF OTHERS
ONE → 30
TWO → 35
THREE → 28
FOUR → 18
FIVE → 10

24 — THE HEAVENLY HIGHWAY
START
ONE → 27
TWO → 25
THREE → 15
FOUR → 11
FIVE → 10
SIX → 6

16 — RUDRA – BLACK FREEDOM
TWO → 34

8 — THE TEMPORARY HELLS OR "HELL FOR A DAY"
ONE → 27
TWO → 19
THREE → 14
FOUR → 11
FIVE → 10
SIX → 6

Commentaries to the Squares

1

Vajra Hell

Crossed double vajras bar your exit from this very special hell. This is the destination of those who abuse the tantric path, who break their tantric vows through distraction or selfishness. Here the fierce dharma protectors turn upon one in wrath. This is a hell of the most frightful demonic images, the most fearful hell, for its suffering is paranoia rather than physical pain —difficult for anyone else to assuage. Fear for oneself makes it almost impossible to see through the images and escape.

> To become my disciple you must observe the precepts,
> Violate not the rules of Vajrayāna,
> Debase not the great Compassion,
> Afflict not the body, word, and mind of Buddhists.
> If you ever violate these rules
> You can be assured of plummeting to the Vajra Hell!
>
> —*Milarepa*

After throwing:
    "One" once,
    "two" twice,
    "three" three times,
    "four" four times,
    "five" five times, and
    "six" six times,
    Go to the realm of Yama, Lord of the Dead (No. 9).

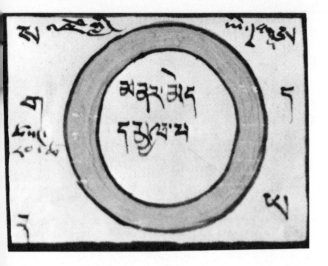

2

Interminable Hell

Falling upside down for two thousand years, one reaches the deepest and hottest of the hells. The others seem idyllic by comparison, for the sufferings here follow one another without intermission.

The Avīci Hell is a prison of incandescent iron. Flames beat against the sides. The gates open and close to frustrate the inhabitants. Some are boiled in iron kettles of molten bronze, "head down like the ingredients of rice soup."

This inverted place of torture represents the complete pollution of the world by malicious confusion and perverse, ego-centered drive. Such a state is created by activities that undermine the basis of civilized life: the murder of one's parents, teacher, or holy personage; cutting off the water supply of a nation; and, especially, destruction of the Dharma or the Buddhist community, for this is a blow to the chances of others for spiritual advancement—the worst of crimes, and the very opposite of a bodhisattva's conduct.

After throwing:

    "One," go to the Southern Continent (No. 17);
    "two," become a Hungry Ghost (No. 10);
    "three," go to the Hot Hells (No. 3).

3

The Hot and Very Hot Hells

In these adjoining torture chambers, one suffers the tortures of intense heat. The *ordinary* Hot Hell is the karmic creation of those who have committed crimes involving fire, such as incendiary action or killing living creatures in a forest fire. Molten bronze is poured through one's mouth, burning away the intestines. One's anus is pierced through to the crown of the head with thorny, one-spiked weapons.

The *very* Hot Hell is a result of the general activities of the milder hells—killing, stealing, sexual abuse, and lying—associated with the intentional perversion of truth. Quack doctors, for example, are found here. However, this is the special destiny of offenders against spiritual practice: stealing food from yogis, raping nuns or virtuous laywomen, seducing monks, or persuading people to disbelieve in karma with any sort of perverse doctrine. This would include the professional tempting of people into harmful or unprofitable paths. In the main hall of this hell, fierce demons with huge black bellies, flaming eyes, and hooked fangs drag the offender into lakes of fire studded with iron spikes.

After throwing:

"One," become an Animal (No. 11);
"two," become a Hungry Ghost (No. 10);
"three," go to the Temporary Hells (No. 8);
"four," go to the Cold Hells (No. 7);
"five," go to the Rope and Crushing Hells (No. 5);
"six," go to the Interminable Hell (No. 2).

4

The Howling and Great Howling Hells

The sins of these two hells both involve misuse of the mouth: the improper use of intoxicants and lying. In consequence, demons fill one's mouth with molten copper, which destroys one's insides.

Drunkenness is not of itself a misdeed, but by becoming so intoxicated with alcohol that one breaks another of the vows—by killing, stealing, or abusing sexuality—one falls laughing, it is said, into the Howling Hell. Especially, the sale of liquor for profit or its use for the harmful manipulation of others gives rise to this bad karma.

The Great Howling Hell arises from lying or harsh speech with spiteful intention: perjury, bribery, betrayal of trust, false advertising, and venal government or justice. One who has lied while quarreling with a companion has his tongue grow to great length. Demons then dig in it a deep ditch, which is filled with molten copper; worms are born in its sides, which devour the tongue.

After throwing:

 "One," become a Nāga (No. 13);
 "two," become a Hungry Ghost (No. 10);
 "three," go to the Temporary Hells (No. 8);
 "four," go to Reviving Hell (No. 6);
 "five," go to the Rope and Crushing Hells (No. 5);
 "six," go to the Hot Hells (No. 3).

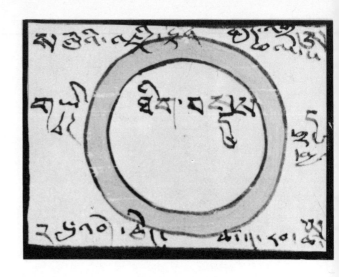

5

The Black Rope
and Crushing Hells

These two hot hells are created by those who violate the second and third guides to lay conduct: stealing and improper sexuality. The offense must have been compounded with murder, for all the hellish states have malice as their cause, whether against life or the killing of spiritual possibilities.

The Black Rope Hell is for thieves—those who have taken what is not offered, or appropriated more than their fair share at the expense of others. The victim is caught by demons and bound to the ground with charcoal-blackened cords. His body is sliced along the markings with fiery saws and axes until it is shredded to bits.

The "Crushing" or "Crowded" Hell is for malicious sexual offenders. Their torture is to be crushed between iron mountains until they revive; then they are crushed again. In one area of this hell one wanders through forests of trees with sharp leaves. At the top of a tree one spies a beautiful and alluring lover from the past. Climbing the tree, the hot leaves destroy one's body, and on reaching the top the phantom lover is heard calling from the ground. At this point the leaves of the tree reverse themselves to point upward. After a painful descent, the image is once again seen above. Blinded by desire born from ignorance, these victims of delusion never cease pursuing and being torn.

After throwing:

　　"One," become a Nāga (No. 13);
　　"two," become an Animal (No. 11);
　　"three," become a Hungry Ghost (No. 10);
　　"four," go to the Cold Hells (No. 7);
　　"five," go to the Howling Hells (No. 4);
　　"six," go to the Hot Hells (No. 3).

6

Reviving Hell

One has fallen into the first of eight hot hells, this one reserved for killers. For the intentional murder of living beings—as through warfare—whether directly or by removing the requisites for life, one suffers here by being tied to others. A string of people murder one another, then are revived by a cool wind to kill and be killed again until their karma is exhausted.

One of the neighborhoods of this hell contains hunters who remorselessly have killed birds or deer for food. Here, in the "place of excrement," they are forced to eat a kind of dung filled with worms whose beaks are diamond hard; they are then themselves devoured from inside.

> People who kill living beings,
> out of greed, stupidity, anger, or fear,
> or raise them for the slaughter,
> must go to Reviving Hell.

After throwing:

"One," go to the Southern Continent (No. 17);
"two," become a Divine Animal (No. 12);
"three," become a Hungry Ghost (No. 10);
"four," go to the Temporary Hells (No. 8);
"five," go to the Rope and Crushing Hells (No. 5);
"six," go to the Howling Hells (No. 4).

7
The Cold Hells

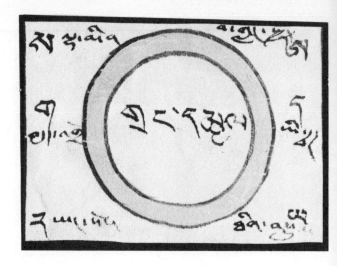

One suffers now in the Cold Hells beneath the earth, parallel to the infernos. As with all hellish states, this is the result of hateful activity—in particular, of crimes against the Dharma from within. There are eight cold hells, their names being sufficient indication of their nature.

arbuda—blistering;

nirarbuda—broken blisters;

atata—chattering teeth;

hahava—where the mouth is frozen and one can only groan;

huhuva—where no articulate sound at all is possible;

utpala—like the blue lotus, where one has a greenish-blue color and one's flesh splits in six petals;

padma—like the red ten-petaled lotus;

mahāpadma or *puṇḍarīka*—like the thousand-petaled lotus.

After throwing:

"One," become an Asura (No. 15);

"two," go to the Western Continent (No. 18);

"three," become an Animal (No. 11);

"four," become a Hungry Ghost (No. 10);

"five," go to Reviving Hell (No. 6);

"six," go to the Rope and Crushing Hells (No. 5).

8

The Temporary Hells, or "Hell for a Day"

This is hell on earth—isolated places such as a river, mountain, or desert. Whereas the lower hells have been created by the collective karma of all living beings, these are innumerable and individualized, created by individual or group activities.

After throwing:

"One," go to the Realm of the Four Great Kings (No. 27);
"two," go to the Eastern Continent (No. 19);
"three," go to Demon Island (No. 14);
"four," become an Animal (No. 11);
"five," go to the Cold Hells (No. 7);
"six," go to Reviving Hell (No. 6).

9

Lord of the Dead (Yama)

With great power and cruelty one has become Yama (or his sister Yamī), lord and judge of the dead, or one of his police demons (yama-rākṣasa). His court is the gateway to hell. Ordinary persons must confront him when they die, gazing into his mirror of karma. Yama has the face of a buffalo, and a buffalo is his mount. His right hand holds a club known as "the punisher," the top of which is a skull. His left hand makes a threatening gesture with a noose. He blazes like the fire that consumes the world at the end of the age.

Yama's world is beneath the earth where the sun never shines, beneath blackish red and green clouds; a dark iron castle without doors surrounded by lakes of gore from which fierce spirits, blazing with hatred, are spontaneously produced.

Beneath Yama himself a monkey-headed demon holds a set of scales on which white and black pebbles, representing one's good and bad deeds, determine one's destiny. After judgment, fierce police demons seize the defendant and lead him upward or downward to his next rebirth.

The ugly demons of Yama's retinue, male and female, have come into this state through avarice and jealousy. They may have been wicked kings or government agents in their previous lives. It is not the case, however, that the torturers of hell, under his command, are living creatures themselves, for if they were living beings they would also experience the sufferings—the extreme heat, and so forth—of the hells. Rather, they are a part of the karmic delusion of the poor hell-beings.

Yama himself has a subjective aspect, being the personification of the inevitable judgment of an individual's deeds, and a concealed, or inner, aspect in that he is inherent in consciousness that is defiled by desire, hatred, and ignorance. In this square he is called "karmic Yama" to show that the external Lord of the Dead is intended.

After throwing:

"One," go to Tantra, Greater Path of Accumulation (No. 42);
"two," go to Mahākāla (No. 34).

10

Hungry Ghosts (Preta)

Just under the earth—and roving upon it—are these creatures, tormented by greed. Their senses are distorted, and the earth seems without sustenance. They have mouths like pins, bellies like mountains, and throats that turn food to fire. Rivers of water take on the appearance of pus or blood. Rushing to a phantasmagoric banquet, they are beaten away by fierce warriors. Fruit trees seem to turn them away with thorny branches. Others among them, who have stolen out of greed or regretted making offerings, are forced to live on vomit or excrement.

Pretas can only be nourished by faith—that is, by offerings made in the course of a religious ceremony and then consigned to them.

After throwing:

"One," go to the Eastern Continent (No. 19);
"two," become a Nāga (No. 13);
"three," go to Demon Island (No. 14);
"four," become an Animal (No. 11);
"five," go to the Temporary Hells (No. 8);
"six," go to the Howling Hells (No. 4).

11

Animals

Residing mostly in the great oceans, animals are created as a result of previous stupidity—intentional ignorance. Guided by their instinctual reactions, they have, for the most part, no intelligence or will. If domestic, they are bound to servitude; if wild, they are doomed to be killed for the sake of their bodies. Generally they must suffer to eat whatever comes near their mouths.

The serpent is said to be born from anger, the lion from pride, the dog from arrogance, the monkey from greed, the crow from insolence, venomous types from having been animal killers, the carnivore from greed and anger, and the horse from unpaid debts.

After throwing:

"One," go to the Realm of the Four Great Kings (No. 27);
"two," go to the Southern Continent (No. 17);
"three," become a Divine Animal (No. 12);
"four," become a Nāga (No. 13);
"five," become a Hungry Ghost (No. 10);
"six," go to the Rope and Crushing Hells (No. 5).

12

Divine Animals

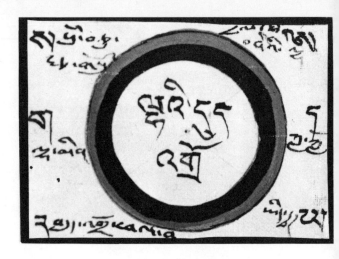

One is born a mythological beast endowed with supernatural powers. These animals are "divine" because their birth is miraculous, like that of a god, and not from a womb or an egg. Some are pets of the gods—the swans, peacocks, bees, and stags populating the gardens of the heavens. These live in a state of radiance, enjoying the pleasures of the heavens but without any sharp intelligence, and are said to be former sculptors and painters who donated their services to the community. Others are mounts of the gods, such as the nāgas (No. 13) and garudas—huge birds with the trunk of a human being and the deadly enemies of the nāga-serpents. Gandharvas, "fragrance eaters," are celestial musicians, born for their great love of flowers. Still others are demigods under the command of the gods. The demigods reside in mountains or trees and become the object of local cults, very powerful in comparison to ordinary creatures but often monstrous and malformed—the karmic result of liberality mixed with a violent nature. These yakṣas and kumbhāṇḍas can bestow good or ill on humanity depending on their disposition.

After throwing:

"One," go to the Heaven of the Thirty-three (No. 28);
"two," go to the Realm of the Four Great Kings (No. 27);
"three," become an Asura (No. 15);
"four," go to Barbarism (No. 21);
"five," become an Animal (No. 11);
"six," become a Hungry Ghost (No. 10).

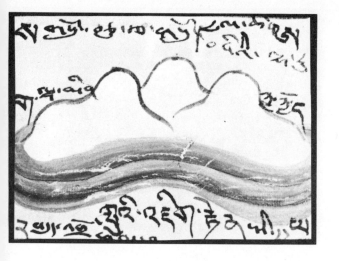

13
World of the Nāgas

These water serpents are human from the waist up, rather like mer creatures. They are spirits of the underworld, to be found at points where their realm impinges on ours—such as springs and rivers. They store great treasures of wealth and precious stones, and sometimes books of secret teachings in underwater palaces. Like other wealthy beings, however, they are dangerous and volatile. Benign nāgas can be the most generous of allies, but their fierce counterparts are known to cause certain classes of disease. In Tibet they are propitiated as lords of the rain.

The powerful nāgas were formerly people very generous in temperament, but also angry and cruel. Their deadly enemy is the garuda, strongest of the birds.

After throwing:

    "One," go to the Heaven of the Thirty-three (No. 28);
    "two," go to the Realm of the Four Great Kings (No. 27);
    "three," become an Asura (No. 15);
    "four," go to Barbarism (No. 21);
    "five," become an Animal (No. 11);
    "six," become a Hungry Ghost (No. 10).

14

Demon Island

These ferocious man-eating demons (rākṣasas) frequent the night—haunting cemeteries, attacking people, and devouring children. Their figures are blood-red; they ride a red ass with a white belly called a *bong-bu,* swift as the wind. With supernormal powers they can take any shape. Demon Island is identified as Srī Lanka, southeast of India. These demons plagued Tibet in ancient times until they were bound by Padmasambhava to the Dharma. Their karmic inheritance derives from the pitiless murder of animals for the benefit of others. From killing they become monstrous and malformed; from giving to others they grow powerful.

After throwing:

"One," begin the Tantric Path (No. 25);
"two," go to Tantra, Greater Accumulation (No. 42);
"three," go to the Southern Continent (No. 17);
"four," become an Asura (No. 15);
"five," go to the Rope and Crushing Hells (No. 5);
"six," go to the Hot Hells (No. 3).

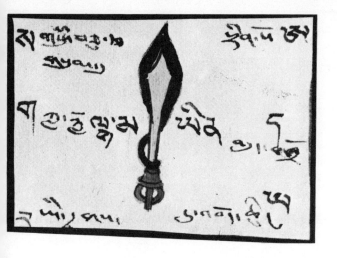

15

Asuras

One is born among the "antigods," so known for their intense jealousy of the gods of thirty-three (No. 28) who got them drunk and cast them out of heaven. The asuras are proud, envious, angry, and warlike. They envy the gods their riches, especially the fruits of the wish-granting tree whose roots are in their realm but that flowers high up in the deva realms on Mount Meru. Unable to defeat the gods in battle, they attempt to cut down the tree.

The asuras live in a "city of light." One asura king named Rāhu is responsible for eclipses, periodically swallowing the sun or the moon. They are also associated with storms, earthquakes, comets, meteors, and other astral phenomena. As for the karma that results in this state, the verse says:

> Ever deceitful and deluding,
> he does no other harm;
> fond of quarreling, yet generous,
> he'll become an asura lord.

After throwing:
   "One," go to the Heaven of the Thirty-three (No. 28);
   "two," go to Demon Island (No. 14);
   "three," go to Barbarism (No. 21);
   "four," become an Animal (No. 11);
   "five," become a Hungry Ghost (No. 10);
   "six," go to the Howling Hells (No. 4).

16

Rudra Black Freedom

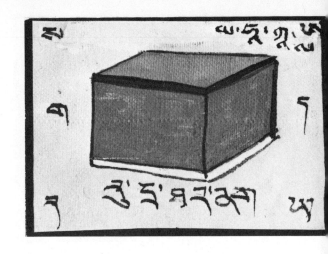

This is the criminal yogi, who accomplishes the worldly occult powers (siddhi)—pacifying, prospering, subjugating, and destroying—from a desire for power. The state of this demigod Rudra, whose name means "the howler" in Sanskrit, results from practicing the tantras without a firm commitment to the welfare of others.

"Rudra" is a name for the god Shiva, and the story of Evil Freedom is the explanation of how this god-as-bully came to exist. There was once a bodhisattva tantrist known as Prince Unassailable. Two men, the first named "Kau Ensnared," whose dharma name became Black Freedom (Mokṣakāla), and his servant Brahmadeva, applied to him for instruction. The servant understood well the import of the secret teachings and kept his vows; but the other took the tantras as an excuse for self-indulgence, broke his vows with all sorts of hideous activities, and expelled the other. When he died he was hurled into lower states of rebirth for many ages, finally appearing as the fierce non-Buddhist god Rudra. His mother died at birth and the townspeople, frightened at his appearance, buried him with her. Feeding on her flesh, he emerged to lead an army of demons in conquest of the world. His former teacher and fellow student, having meanwhile attained great powers within the Dharma, took the forms of a horse (the fierce Hayagrīva) and a boar (the diamond sow) and subjugated him.

A parallel story shows Shiva, "lord of the world," being bound by the fierce bodhisattva Vajrapaṇi to become Mahākāla, a Dharma protector.

Rudra is the god of the type of yogi whose accomplishments are based on ego gratification (ātma-vāda). His "liberation" is a form of claustrophobia—imprisonment in the self-made coffin of his ego. He fancies himself the creator and lord of the universe, and is the prototype of the jealous god who must attempt to control everything around him. Hence Shiva's religion is that of power and fear, known in India as linga worship. Stories of his destructive pride are numerous. The god of love, in Indian mythology, has no body because Rudra burned it with a glance from his third eye, in vengeance for disturbing his meditations. An asura king who made offerings to him reluctantly, placing him among the last rank of the gods, had all his temple and offerings destroyed by fire and was only able to placate the god by giving up his daughter Parvatī.

Rudra is placed here in the last rank of the gods, and just above the less powerful asuras. His only escape from himself is conversion by a tantric bodhisattva.

After throwing:
  "Two," become Mahākāla (No. 34).

17

Jambu Island—
The Southern Continent

One has the great fortune to be born in a human condition on earth. This situation is a mixed bag to be sure, for there are such hells on earth as sickness, warfare, and poverty. Yet it is the luckiest birth among the karmic destinies, for only a human being has these three things: the stimulus to seek an escape from the cycle of death and rebirth, the opportunity to encounter the Dharma, and the leisure to study and practice it. In addition, this is said to be the only continent on which the Buddha will demonstrate the way to nirvana, "because the inhabitants of Jambu Island have a sharp intelligence."

This continent, south of Mount Meru, is named after the mythic rose-apple (jambu) tree. Trapezoidal in shape "like a chariot," its center is the diamond seat (vajrāsana) at Bodhgaya, on which the Buddha demonstrates the way of Awakening.

After throwing:

"One," begin the Mahāyāna, Lesser Accumulation (No. 52);
"two," begin the Tantric Path (No. 25);
"three," become a Wheel-Turning King (No. 26);
"four," begin the Vehicle of the Disciples (No. 38);
"five," go to Hinduism (No. 22);
"six," go to Reviving Hell (No. 6).

18

The Western Continent— Enjoyment of Cattle (Apara-Godānīya)

Here is the fortunate human existence and great enjoyment of wealth in a land of lakes and pastures. The Dharma is present here but it does not flourish, for the inhabitants are rough and live only by eating meat. Certain traditions record that the people here experience synesthesia—the eye hears sounds, for example, and the ear sees colors—and that they perform the sex act only some ten or twelve times in the course of their lives.

Godānīya has a red tone in its skies and waters, the reflection of the ruby western walls of Mount Meru.

After throwing:

"One," enter the Vehicle of the Disciples (No. 38);
"two," go to the Realm of the Four Great Kings (No. 27);
"three," become a Nāga (No. 13);
"four," go to Barbarism (No. 21);
"five," become an Animal (No. 11);
"six," become a Hungry Ghost (No. 10).

19

The Eastern Continent—
Noble Figure
(Pūrva-Videha)

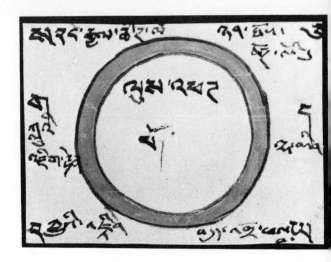

One has an especially fine and noble human form on the continent east of Mount Meru. Here the light is bright and clear from the crystal wall of the mountain, and the people tranquil and mild.

After throwing:

"One," begin the Vehicle of the Independent Buddha (No. 43);

"two," begin the Vehicle of the Disciples (No. 38);

"three," become a Nāga (No. 13);

"four," become an Asura (No. 15);

"five," become a Nāga (No. 13);

"six," become an Animal (No. 11).

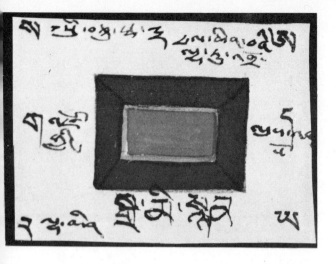

20
The Northern-Continent— Kuru

This continent, shaded green by the emerald north face of Mount Meru, is the happiest of the four human islands. The people lead a wholesome communal existence. There is no private property or marriage, and they are undisturbed by desires or aggressiveness. According to ancient tradition, the women nurse through their fingers, and the children are brought up in common—boys by the men, girls by the women.

Little work is required for subsistence: Corn ripens of its own accord, and fragrant rice is found boiling on the stoves; the trees are always in foliage and fruit. Because they are not in the habit of declaring "This is mine," and so forth, these people are incapable of the worst crimes and suffer no untimely death, living out their full life spans of a thousand years. Upon dying they do not enter the three lowest destinies.

Nonetheless, this idyllic sort of existence is said to be not conducive to the paths to liberation. Like the gods, the people of Kuru cannot keep religious vows. No saint develops here, for they never come to understand the initial postulate of the Dharma: Life is basically suffering. Their faculties are dulled by their uneventful lives, and they are incapable of difficult meditations. In short, they create no bad karma, but neither do they make progress toward liberation from sàmsāra.

After throwing:

  "One," go to the Heaven of the Thirty-three (No. 28);
  "two," go to the Realm of the Four Great Kings (No. 27);
  "three," go to the Southern Continent (No. 17);
  "four," go to the Eastern Continent (No. 19);
  "five," become an Asura (No. 15).

21

Barbarism

One is born a human being, but in an uncivilized and materialistic society in which warfare is considered the legitimate mode of human interaction. The mountains are pictured as rocky and reddened with blood. This is the karmic result of cruelty, fighting, and pitiless meat-eating.

In particular, barbarism refers to the Muslim Turkish tribes who swept into India from Central Asia and, being iconoclasts by ideology, destroyed the images, books, and communities of the holy Dharma. In Lhasa they formed the profession of butchers. In general this state indicates barbarity —any philosophy that rationalizes intolerance and warfare.

It is acknowledged that in India there occurred an amalgamation of Hindu and Muslim faiths; hence one can rise from here to the top of the Hindu path.

After throwing:

"One," become an Asura (No. 15);
"two," go to Hindu Wisdom-Master (No. 62);
"three," become a Nāga (No. 13);
"four," become an Animal (No. 11);
"five," become a Hungry Ghost (No. 10);
"six," go to Interminable Hell (No. 2).

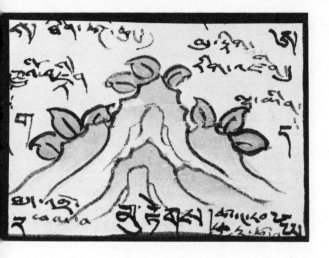

22

Hinduism

With moderately good fortune one is born into the brahmanical culture of India, pictured as a green and fruitful land. Here civilization is rich and vigorous, the arts and sciences flourish, and metaphysical speculation is highly advanced. Life here is so full that one tends to adopt an extreme, externalistic view. There exists an abiding principle to man and the world. Although conceptions such as "God" and "the soul" provide a superficial consistency to the world, inspire an exalted ethical code, and stimulate meditative accomplishments, they are ultimately unverifiable and unable to bear scrutiny by logic, and furthermore become a source of bondage to sàmsāra, inspiring misguided and harmful practices such as religious sacrifice and ascetic self-mutilation.

Nonetheless, this rich culture is the birthplace of the true Dharma and the holy land of Buddhism.

After throwing:

"One," begin the Mahāyāna, Lesser Accumulation (No. 52);

"two," go to Hindu Wisdom-Holder (No. 62);

"three," become a Nāga (No. 13);

"four," become an Asura (No. 15);

"five," become an Animal (No. 11);

"six," go to the Hot Hells (No. 3).

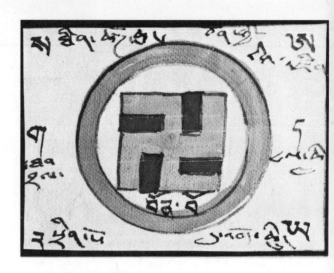

23
Bön

Bön (pronounced "pern") is shamanism or sorcery in a highly developed form. In Tibet it represents the alternative to Buddhism. Bön antedates the Dharma, having come from the direction of Persia in the early centuries A.D. There are close analogies with other shamanic traditions, such as Taoism. The ancient kings of Tibet were considered sky gods (btsan-po). They were sorcerers, able to travel at will by a heavenly rope or riding a drum among the three realms: the underworld, earth, and sky. The sorcerer is expert in communicating with spirits; his trades are weathermaking, divination, and funeral ritual, for he can guide the spirit after death.

Modern Bön, on the other hand, has adopted Buddhist scriptures to its own system, and is virtually a replica of the Old School of Tibetan Buddhism. But the bön-po reverse the Buddhist auspicious emblem, the swastika, and circumambulate sacred places counterclockwise, which causes their fellow Tibetans no end of merriment. In comparison with the other non-Buddhist traditions in this game, Bön is considered to have the greatest potential for spiritual progress.

After throwing:

"One," begin the Mahāyāna, Lesser Accumulation (No. 52);

"two," go to Bön, Wisdom-Holder (No. 65);

"three," go to the Heaven Without Fighting (No. 29);

"four," go to the Realm of the Four Great Kings (No. 27);

"five," go to Demon Island (No. 14);

"six," go to the Howling Hells (No. 4).

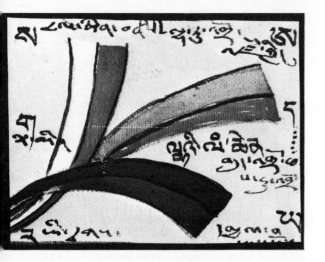

24

The Heavenly Highway

We are at the start of the game, in the present human existence, confronted with six roads of different colors. The fall of the die takes us to one of the six karmic destinies: white for the gods, blue for humans, green for animals, yellow for ghosts, black smoke for the hells, and red for the jealous asuras. But karma is not fate; it means activity. Deeds of body, speech, and mind will determine our destination.

> The opportunity has arrived, so hard to obtain,
> for accomplishing the welfare of living beings;
> If I fail to take advantage of it,
> When will the chance come again?

After throwing:

"One," go to the Realm of the Four Great Kings (No. 27);
"two," go to the Southern Continent (No. 17);
"three," become an Asura (No. 15);
"four," become an Animal (No. 11);
"five," become a Hungry Ghost (No. 10);
"six," go to Reviving Hell (No. 6).

25

Beginning the Tantra

One sets forth toward enlightenment in the vehicle of mantra, the diamond path, the secret way of the practice of spells (vidyā). This is the way of the elite and the shortcut up the mountain to Buddhahood.

If one came here as a demon, one has been bound to the Dharma by the compassionate force of a tantric master; if one came as a human being, the key is a qualified guru or lama, for among the Buddhist paths this is the dangerous way and the most strenuous and disciplined technique.

The mark of a qualified lama is that he or she at the very least keeps his or her own vows. Without the proper commitments this road leads to madness and hell. In addition to the three vows of the Mahāyāna—refuge in the Three Jewels (Buddha, Dharma, and community), that of the bodhisattva (to save all beings), and that of lay or monastic conduct—tantric practice requires a set of fourteen "root" and eight "branch" precepts that guide not only physical action but thought and speech as well.

In the beginning stages one practices the bodhisattva path in an intensive form, combining the thought of enlightenment (the bodhisattva vow) with devotional commitment and meditative purification. In particular one practices the four common (mahāyānist) and the four special (tantric) preliminaries. The former set consists of a week's meditation on each of four thoughts, which turn the mind toward Awakening: the value of human birth, death and impermanence, the cause-and-effect pattern of karma, and the horrors of sàmsāra. These being well learned, there follow the special tantric preliminaries: one hundred thousand repetitions of each of four ritual meditations designed to establish a firm foundation for further practice. These are the vows of refuge and the bodhisattva resolution, the purification mantra of Vajrasattva, the mandala offering to the sources of refuge, and visualized union with one's lineage of gurus.

In this way one accomplishes the equivalent of the Mahāyāna Path of Accumulation in the space of a few months or years. As is usual in Buddhism, knowledge comes only in conjunction with meditative experience and ability.

After throwing:

"One," go to Wisdom-Holder of the Eight Siddhis (No. 72);
"two," go to Tantra, Lesser Accumulation (No. 33);
"six," begin the Vehicle of the Disciples (No. 38).

26

Wheel-Turning King (Cakravartin)

The great monarch of mankind unites the entire world under a righteous government. The wheel of authority, perhaps to be identified with the roving chariots of the conquerors of old, appears like the sun in the eastern sky of his youth.

There are four types of wheel—gold, silver, copper, and iron—which rule, respectively, over four, three, two, and one continents. Petty kings beg to submit to the golden-wheeled ruler, the lord of the silver wheel goes to them; the copper king prepares for war, the iron brandishes arms. In any case, the Cakravartin never slays. Through the previous accumulation of merit—generosity, the appreciation of others, and especially the complete absence of anger—he enters the womb, like the Buddha-to-be, in complete awareness of the situation, and emerges physically resplendent. He cannot be killed by himself or by others, nor can his mother be slain while pregnant with him.

Seven precious articles benefit the rule of the Cakravartin: the faultless and wonderful queen, the magic protective jewel, the conquering wheel, the great elephant, the swift horse, the righteous general, and the wise minister. Seven minor possessions are also the best of their kind: sword, hide tent, bed, garden, palaces, robes, and boots. The Cakravartin has great physical strength as well as the "divine eye": the vision of past and future lives.

The dynasty of wheel-turning kings appears just after the golden age of the world (which is harmonious anarchy, with no need of government). As the Buddhist ideal of the state, it presents some analogies with that of Plato's *Republic*. The ruler, whose status is the consequence of good conduct as a human, protects his citizenry and establishes them on the wholesome paths of activity. The closest to a Cakravartin among rulers of history was Aśoka of the Maurya Dynasty (third century B.C.), who governed India in accordance with the Dharma.

After throwing:

　　"One," go to the Heaven Without Fighting (No. 29);
　　"two," go to the Heaven of the Thirty-three (No. 28);
　　"three," go to the Southern Continent (No. 17);
　　"four," go to the Northern Continent (No. 20);
　　"five," become a Nāga (No. 13);
　　"six," become a Nāga (No. 13).

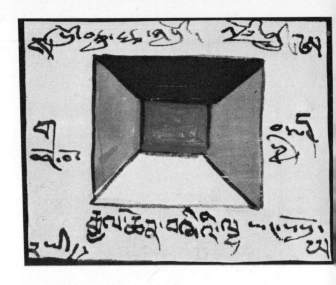

27

Heaven of the
Four Great Kings

One is born into the broadly based lower classes of divinity who rule the lower slopes of Mount Meru, the seven chains of mountains around it, and the skies. These deities regulate the mundane affairs of the world system. The four kings each take one direction, looking out from the sides of Mount Meru over the realms beneath, and protecting the Gods of the Thirty-three, above them, from attacks by the asuras.

The four kings are regents for the higher gods over the world; the armies and messengers of the kings are the spirits of water, trees, mountains, and so forth. Some among these gods are associated with the planetary bodies, in the astrological sense of regulators of the world. The kings appear outside the doorways of temples, being transformed from world protectors (loka-pāla) into defenders of the faith (dharma-pāla).

Dhṛtarāṣṭra, lord of gandharvas (the celestial musicians), rules the East; Virūpākṣa, lord of the monstrous kumbhāṇḍas, rules the South; Virūpāksa, lord of nāgas, rules the West; and Vaiśravaṇa, lord of yakṣa demigods, rules the North. The last is widely worshiped as Kuvera, lord of wealth; he carries in his arms the jewel-spitting mongoose.

The *apsaras,* goddesses of this realm, give birth in a miraculous manner, free of the burdens of menstruation, pregnancy, confinement, and nursing. The child is born (appearing on its mother's knees or hip) at five years of age, and the gods or goddesses think, "This is our son," or "This is our daughter." The child in turn conceives the thought, "These are our fathers," or "These are our mothers." Thus they grow up with collective parenthood, freed from association with sexuality. During copulation the deities of this level unite their bodies but without emission of substance or loss of energy. As is the case with all the deva gods, sexuality is casual and easily repeated.

The status of these beings is the result of neither aspiring to selfish happiness and goods nor exulting in their possession.

After throwing:
"One," go to the Heaven of the Thirty-three (No. 28);
"two," go to the Southern Continent (No. 17);
"three," go to Bön (No. 23);
"four," go to the Western Continent (No. 18);
"five," become a Hungry Ghost (No. 10);
"six," go to Reviving Hell (No. 6).

28

Heaven of the Thirty-three
(Trāyātriṁśa)

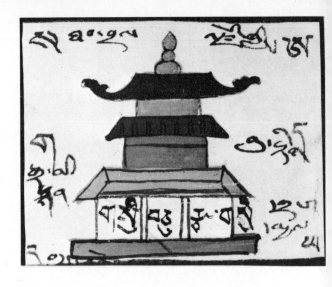

One dwells in a region, at the summit of Mount Meru, with thirty-three divine neighborhoods. The devas of this level are large and powerful, with supernatural sensory faculties. Chief among them is Indra, the old warrior god of vedic times, now a dharma protector who owes his high karmic status to reverence and generosity toward the Buddha. These gods, like their Greek counterparts on Olympus, are not quite beyond the affairs of the world. Their realm was won from the asuras and must be periodically defended. Hence it is surrounded by a wall of gold.

The ground of this heaven is rainbow-colored, soft, and yielding to the foot. At the four corners of the mountain are peaks guarded by *vajrapāṇi*, "thunderbolt handed" yakṣas. The central peak is Indra's city Sudarśana, meaning "belleview." Four parks with magic lakes grace its sides, each with playgrounds beside it containing soft and lovely soil.

To the northeast within Sudarśana is the tall magnolia known as Pārijā-taka, "full-grown," whose incense spreads to all quarters, even against the wind; its shade is the perfect spot for the pleasures of music and love. The divinities of this realm couple by merely touching together their sexual organs. Southwest is Sudharma, "good Dharma," the divine meeting hall for affairs of state. In the center is Indra's jeweled palace Vaijayanta, "the Conqueror's."

Although these gods take their refuge in the Buddha, their pleasure is too great to allow for religious practice. In consequence, they are unable to prevent rebirth in a lower state when good karma is exhausted. There is said to be no greater suffering than that of a dying god who can foresee his or her future rebirth. The approach of a divine fall has five signs: one's dress becomes soiled, flower garlands fade, perspiration clouds the armpits, the body emits an unpleasant smell, and one's seat becomes uncomfortable. With this, one's companions and lovers desert one in disgust. Indra is said to have a gallery of portraits of past kings of this region, depicting their fall and rebirth. The misery that signals the end of this happy state is taken to provide final proof of the necessity of ending suffering entirely by overcoming the very process of death and rebirth.

After throwing:
"One," go to the Heaven Without Fighting (No. 29);
"two," go to the Southern Continent (No. 17);
"three," go to the Northern Continent (No. 20);
"four," go to Hinduism (No. 22);
"five," become an Animal (No. 11);
"six," go to the Cold Hells (No. 7).

29

Heaven Without Fighting
(Yāma)

Even larger and more powerful than the Gods of the Thirty-three, the Yāma devas are completely beyond the strife of the world and secure in their possession of heaven. Their paradise hangs in space like a cloud bank, twice as high above sea level as the peak of Mount Meru. The seeds of their past moral conduct, the essence of which is self-control and avoidance of conflict, blossom into the delights of the Realm of Desire: gardens of lakes, swans, water lilies, and sexual enjoyment that is consummated by a mere embrace. Pictured is the wish-granting jewel, symbolizing their possession of whatever one might desire.

Among the bodhisattvas in residence here is the king of swans, Suyāma, who lives in the heart of a huge lotus. His role is to warn the gods against distraction, so that they may not fall into a lower state at death. At one point Māra, lord of the Realm of Desire, sent down three messengers —Delight, Distraction, and Confusion—to protest this threat to his prerogatives. There ensued an extended discussion of the Dharma, and they returned defeated, unable to shake the devas of this realm.

After throwing:

  "One," go to the Joyful Heaven (No. 30);
  "two," go to Delighting in Emanations (No. 31);
  "three," go to the Southern Continent (No. 17);
  "four," go to Bön (No. 23);
  "five," become a Divine Animal (No. 12);
  "six," become a Hungry Ghost (No. 10).

The Joyful (Tuṣita) Heaven

Although only the fourth of six heavens in the realm of sense desire, this is the most promising for one's future, for it is traditionally the penultimate abode of the bodhisattva, the station before his final birth in human form. The future Buddha Maitreya, "loving one," is presently in residence in Tuṣita, under the pseudonym "savior god" (nātha-deva).

Tuṣita is the most beautiful of all the deva realms. A newborn Tibetan child has reported that the inhabitants drink nectar (amṛta), that the flowers are white and grand, and that the buildings, even the earth, are strewn with jewels. This mansion, floating high above Mount Meru like a cloud, is the favorite resort of Buddhist scholars:

> Erudite persons, upholders of the Dharma,
> the wise ones who are seeking liberation,
> and who delight in learning,
> they go to Tuṣita.

The noble Asaṅga, for example, founder of the Yogācāra or mind-only school, journeyed here for Maitreya's inspiration.

For the ordinary devas of this realm, still bound to sense desires, sexuality is a matter of holding hands.

After throwing:

"One," go to Mahāyāna, Highest Teachings (No. 64);
"two," go to Mahāyāna, Receptivity (No. 63);
"three," go to Mahāyāna, Heat (No. 55);
"four," go to Mahāyāna, Greater Accumulation (No. 54);
"five," go to Mahāyāna, Middle Accumulation (No. 53);
"six," go to Mahāyāna, Lesser Accumulation (No. 52).

Delighting in Emanations (Nirmāṇa-rati)

In this divine mansion, floating high above the summit of Mount Meru, the gods have no need of desirable objects to be present before them, for their very wish becomes reality. So in the process of increasing abstraction represented by the levels of godhead, they are sufficiently detached from the bonds of the material world as to be able to enjoy the emanations of their own minds. Similarly, they enjoy the delights of sexuality by merely laughing together, by conversation, or by inhaling each others' fragrance.

The beings of this heaven emit a brilliant golden light. Their environment is filled with jewels, luxuriant gardens of perfumes and flowers, beautiful plants and creepers, and magnificent trees. From their palaces come the sounds of dancing and music.

The karma giving rise to this state is a sublime moral refinement and intense generosity.

> Persons who proceed by themselves
> and with great will power
> to morality, generosity, and discipline,
> go necessarily to Nirmāṇa-rati.

After throwing:
"One," begin the Mahāyāna, Lesser Accumulation (No. 52);
"two," go to the Joyful Heaven (No. 30);
"three," enter the Vehicle of the Independent Buddhas (No. 43);
"four," go to Ruling Others' Emanations (No. 32);
"five," go to Hinduism (No. 22);
"six," become a Divine Animal (No. 12).

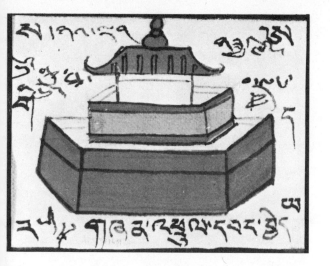

32

*Ruling the Emanations
of Others
(Paranirmita-Vaśavartin)*

In these ethereal mansions, four levels above the summit of Mount Meru, dwell the supreme deities of the world of sense desires.

> Those exalted beings, the very highest,
> who with qualities exceeding all others—
> generosity, self mastery, and control—
> go confidently to Paranirmitahood.

The great prerogative of these gods is that they need no previously existent sense objects to enjoy—nor even, like the gods immediately below them, need they emanate such objects from their own intellect. These great beings rule the emanations of others. Their mental powers are such that whatever they may wish for is anticipated by the other classes of gods, who magically emanate it for their pleasure. The example is given of a cook who will prepare his master's favorite foods.

In this heaven, sexual desire arises and is satisfied by a glance.

The king of this realm is Māra. As lord of the Realm of Desire, this powerful creature is extremely jealous of those who might try to escape it. He sends his armies of pleasant and fearsome distractions to hinder saints and yogis (see No. 100). The successful meditator, passing through his distractions, attains the Realm of Form.

After throwing:

"One," go to the Joyful Heaven (No. 30);
"two," attain the Realm of Form (No. 35);
"three," go to the Heaven of the Thirty-three (No. 28);
"four," go to the Western Continent (No. 18);
"five," become a Hungry Ghost (No. 10).

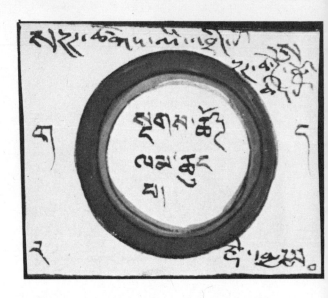

33

Tantra, Lesser Path
of Accumulation

Here, at the beginning of substantial tantric practice, one engages in the tantra of activity (kriya-tantra). Although the highest attainment (siddhi) gained from any tantric meditation is the understanding of the emptiness of all phenomena, the tantras are classified and graded in terms of outer versus inner practice. The activity tantra is especially concerned with the purification of elements of the inner world and the outer world. In it one's self and outer appearances are transformed by the identification of one's ego with the nature of the deity being visualized, one's speech with its mantra, and one's surroundings with its pure land. Thus self and appearances are transmuted in meditation into the loveliness and purity of the Awakened state. If reality is the play of appearances, molded by karma but arising from emptiness, the aim of tantra is its intentional reformation.

According to the Old School, in the activity tantra the deity, a Buddha or bodhisattva, is only visualized in front of one, in the manner of "master and servant." One then takes siddhi from it. The attainments on this level —before one has made the deity one's self—are generally more ordinary than the supreme attainment, Buddhahood. The danger is that one may practice magic without compassion. The rites of subjugation and so forth are based on the mental reformation of reality. By learning them without a proper commitment to the path of helping others, one's selfishness will only be reinforced. Hence this path may lead to the most harrowing of hellish states.

Nonetheless, if done under proper initiation and guidance, the activity tantra, with its emphasis on outer ritual, offerings, and chanting, will accomplish the accumulation of merit. One ideally will make the best sort of offering: one's own concentrated reverence and powers of attention.

> If distracted thoughts still haunt your mind,
> Never claim that you observe the tantric precepts,
> Lest you should fall into the Vajra Hell.

After throwing:

"One," go to Tantra, Middle Accumulation (No. 41);
"two," go to Tantra, Greater Accumulation (No. 42);
"five," go to Rudra (No. 16);
"six," go to Vajra Hell (No. 1).

34

Mahākāla

You have become the "great black one," with aggressive and wrathful energies turned to protect the Dharma. Mahākāla is a world-transcending protector, not bound to the role by force but committed to it by understanding; his third eye indicates that he is a lord of wisdom. He is chief of the ferocious executioners, trampling down any hindrance to meditation or enemy of the Dharma. In the sacred dances he supervises the "liberation" of demons. The powers of Mahākāla may be ritually invoked by the initiate to slay an enemy.

Mahākāla is acknowledged in different forms by each sect (he has some seventy-five forms in Tibet). He is invoked constantly for protection in the secret "lord's house" behind the monastery's altar. Surrounded by flames, he wears an elephant skin on his back and a garland of freshly severed heads. He may be Yama, lord of death, in a new role, or his skull-cup and trident may be considered to make him the great yogi Rudra-Shiva converted to the true Dharma, his ferocious and passionate powers working now to purify the karma of aggression.

After throwing:

   "One," go to Urgyan (No. 61);
   "two," go to the Fifth Tantra Stage (No. 81).
   "three," go to the Realm of Action Completion (No. 70).

35

The Realm of Form
(Rūpa-Dhātu)

Soaring high over Mount Meru beyond the Realm of Sense Desire, these stations of exalted consciousness are the product of "immovable" (aniñja) karma, neither good nor bad. In fact, the seventeen levels of this realm correspond to the subtleties of progress in meditation. With the removal of attachment to the realm of sensory objects and the successful practice of calming meditation (śamatha) comes the possession of an ethereal translucent body, to which neither physical nor mental suffering can adhere.

The first three stages, worlds of the Brahma gods, correspond to the first stage of meditative trance, in which the mind is concentrated on a single thought. These gods in particular have the notion that Brahmā is the great God, the Creator of all.

The second trance causes rebirth among three levels of gods of light (ābha). Here the physical pleasure of meditation fades, giving way to happiness and equanimity. From the third trance comes rebirth as a god of splendor (śubha), again of three levels (weak, middling, and strong degrees of immersion in this trance); these gods experience pleasure and equanimity.

Among the gods of the fourth trance, characterized by equanimity alone, three are included in this square (out of eight; see also No. 37), named "the unclouded," "merit-born," and "great fruition." At the top of this last group is a class of beings totally "thoughtless" (asaṁjñi-sattva).

They themselves mistake their state for nirvana, but it is merely a state of trance and without true knowledge of the world; when a thought at last arises due to their previous karma, they fall back to the Realm of Sense Desire.

After throwing:

"One," go to the Pure Abodes (No. 37);
"two," begin the Mahāyāna, Lesser Accumulation (No. 52);
"three," go to the Formless Realm (No. 36);
"four," go to the Joyful Heaven (No. 30);
"five," go to the Southern Continent (No. 17);
"six," go to the Realm of the Four Great Kings (No. 27).

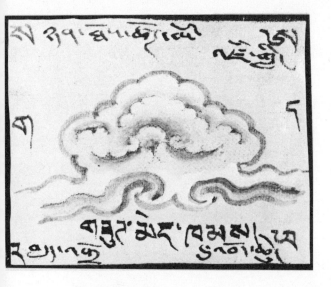

36

The Formless Realm
(Arūpa-Dhātu)

Passing beyond sense desires and then beyond matter, one's mental horizons become so broadened as to encompass endless vistas of space, finally transcending consciousness itself.

There are four meditative "equalizations" (samāpatti) that effect rebirth in the formless or spiritual realm. The four are ranked in order, but, of course, being nonmaterial, they have no "place." Rebirth in them is effected by karma that has no connection with "good" or "bad"—it is a purely mental state without attachment to material elements. The location of these realms is the same as the meditator's last position on earth—at the foot of a tree, for example, in a meditation hall, or in the realm of the gods of form.

The names of the first three levels are based on yogic practices (prayoga).

"1. In contemplating the object of meditation, the yogi transcends all notions of materiality. Hindering concepts set like the sun, and paying no need to notions of multiplicity (ceasing to distinguish the object from its surroundings), he abides thinking 'space is infinite,' so attaining the station of *infinite space.*

"2. Transcending completely the stage of *infinite space,* he considers that 'consciousness is infinite,' and attains and abides in the station of *infinite consciousness.*

"3. Thoroughly transcending the station of *infinite consciousness,* he abides attaining the station of *nothing-at-all,* thinking 'there is nothing at all.'"

The fourth stage involves no concept. "Transcending 'nothing-at-all,' he attains the station of *neither-ideas-nor-the-lack-of-ideas.*" This is called the Peak of Existence. It takes its name from the debility of ideation (samjñā) and not its complete elimination. From this point, however, one can accomplish *nonideation,* and then the equalization called *cessation,* in which the stream of mental events is halted for a period of time. This last stage is sometimes confused with nirvana (cf. No. 48). In these realms, however, attachment to the objects of sense has been eliminated, but there remains attachment to existence. After a period of time, past karma becomes operative and one is reborn in a lower destiny.

After throwing:

   "One," begin the Vehicle of the Disciples (No. 38);
   "two," go to the Southern Continent (No. 17);
   "three," become an Animal (No. 11);
   "six," go to the Howling Hells (No. 4).

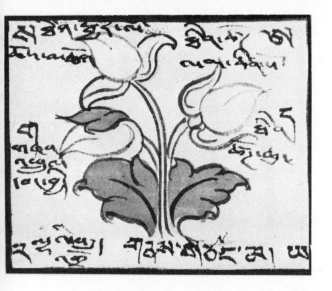

37

Pure Abodes (Śuddhāvāsa)

Here the heights of the Realm of Form are attained by means of the strongest and most concentrated practice of the fourth stage of trance. Five levels of gods abide here, in mansions floating high above Mount Meru. They are classed according to their emphasis on each of the five cardinal virtues: faith, vigor, mindfulness, concentration, and wisdom. The last, called the "unsurpassed" (akaniṣṭha) pure abode, emphasizes wisdom or insight meditation (vipaśyanā). Partaking thus of the nature of enlightenment, this last Akaniṣṭha Realm is not classed here, but at the top of the board (No. 84).

The gods of the Pure Abodes are "virtuous, mighty, long-lived, beautiful, and enjoying great well-being. They are self-luminous, travel through the air, have pleasant food, live happily, and go wheresoever they wish. They are free from passion." Since faith and other virtues besides meditation are involved here, no "ordinary persons" (pṛthagjana) attain to this station, but only āryas, those committed to the Dharma.

After throwing:

"One," go to Mahāyāna, Highest Teachings (No. 64);
"two," go to Mahāyāna, Greater Accumulation (No. 54);
"three," go to Ruling Others' Emanations (No. 32);
"four," go to Mahāyāna, Lesser Accumulation (No. 52);
"five," become a Divine Animal (No. 12).

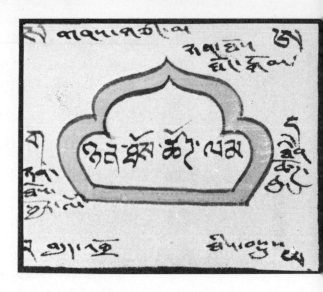

38

Disciples (Śrāvaka),
Path of Accumulation
(Sambhāra-Mārga)

Nurturing a disgust for the cycle of death and rebirth, one enters the Vehicle of the Disciples, beginning to plant wholesome roots conducive to liberation. One takes on the role of a monastic or lay disciple, thus joining the noble family of the Buddhist community. By meditations on the repulsiveness of the body (for the temperament dominated by passion), on dependent origination (to counteract ignorance), on friendliness (antidote to ill will), on breathing (against discursive thought), or on contemplation of the Buddha (counteracting all four), one begins to attack the four perverted views that are deeply ingrained in all ordinary people. These are: seeking permanence in the impermanent, ease in the suffering, the self in what is selfless, and the lovely in what is repulsive. Hence one may attain great meditative advancement. The aim, however, is to gain a degree of mental concentration and to lessen the grossest defilements—attachment, aversion, and bewilderment—that bar the way to freedom.

One accumulates merit through worship and good works, and equips oneself for real practice on the path.

After throwing:
    "One," go to the Pure Abodes (No. 37);
    "two," go to Disciples, Path of Vision (No. 40);
    "three," go to Disciples, Path of Application (No. 39);
    "four," begin the Mahāyāna, Lesser Accumulation (No. 52);
    "five," become an Animal (No. 11);
    "six," go to Rope and Crushing Hells (No. 5).

Disciples, Path of Application (Prayoga-Mārga)

Having accumulated merit and equipped oneself with a degree of meditative ability, one plants wholesome roots conducive to penetration—that is, one applies the benefits from past practice toward the understanding of Dharma. One exercises a higher mindfulness, which takes as its object the Four Noble Truths (see No. 40). In this way, based on the "calm" of meditation, one begins to develop "insight" into the conditioned and impermanent nature of the self. One gains the supreme mental elements of the world, such as the five types of high awareness (abhijñā): (1) wonder-working powers, (2) the heavenly ear, (3) knowledge of others' thoughts, (4) recollection of one's past lives, and (5) insight into the past lives of others. The sixth high awareness—the knowledge that one's outflows are extinct—will come at the end of the road.

If this path is well accomplished, one rises to the world-transcending paths.

After throwing:

"One," begin the Mahāyāna, Lesser Accumulation (No. 52);
"two," begin the Vehicle of the Independent Buddha (No. 43);
"three," go to Disciples, Paths of Vision and Cultivation (No. 40);
"four," begin the Mahāyāna, Lesser Accumulation (No. 52);
"five," go to the Heaven of the Thirty-three (No. 28);
"six," go to the Eastern Continent (No. 19).

40

Disciples, Paths of Vision and Cultivation (Darśana-Mārga, Bhāvanā-Mārga)

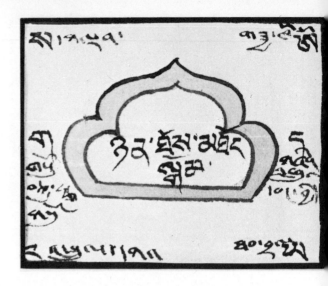

In the course of moral purification and mental concentration, the four noble truths as taught by the Buddha come into view in all their ramifications. One sees that (1) the cycle of rebirth is suffering, (2) the cause of suffering is craving, (3) the elimination of suffering comes from the cessation of attachment, and (4) there is a path to cessation. One abandons the passions that result from doubt, and the view that one's body and mind are possessed and ruled by a central "self." Finally, one abandons attachment to moral codes and ritual. These constitute the Path of Vision.

On the Path of Cultivation the final defilements, which can only be destroyed by hard meditation, are eliminated. The Path of Vision has destroyed the notion of a self; this path destroys the attachment to pleasurable sensation, which persists even after the self is gone. With correct understanding and full concentration, one is able to follow perfectly the Noble Eightfold Path: correctness of views, intentions, speech, conduct, livelihood, effort, mindfulness, and concentration. These being firmly established, one experiences the "diamondlike concentration" (vajropama-samādhi).

After throwing:

"One," go to the Joyful Heaven (No. 30);
"two," go to the Realm of Form (No. 35);
"three," go to the Heaven of the Thirty-three (No. 28);
"four," go to Ruling Others' Emanations (No. 32);
"five," go to Delighting in Emanations (No. 31);
"six," go to the Heaven Without Fighting (No. 29).

114

Tantra, Middle Path of Accumulation

This second class of the tantras is known as "the practice of both" (ubhaya-caryā-tantra), for it combines outer and inner yoga. Again the deity is generated in front of one, but this time "like a brother or a friend." This yoga centers on the chanting of mantras; it is classified as yoga-with-image (union with the visualized deity) and yoga-without-image (union with the deity governed by emptiness). In the former type, while the mantra is repeated, the yogi rests his or her mind in the heart of the deity. Mindfulness of breath (considered "the steed of thought") is practiced to stabilize the meditative image and eliminate discursive thought; thus calm is developed. In the yoga-without-image, one focuses on emptiness; thus insight grows.

Other meditative rituals in this class of tantra procure occult powers through the magical manipulation of objects such as a sword, just as in the Pāli tradition magical powers are attained by meditating on the great elements—earth, air, fire, and water—until their essential nature has been grasped.

The caryā class of tantras is seldom practiced in Tibet; yogis tend to move from the activity tantra to the supreme tantra stage. The chief text of this class is the *Mahā-vairocana,* which is the basis of tantric practice in China and Japan.

> Don't concentrate on yourself, restricting your breath.
> Fie, yogin, don't squint at the end of your nose.
> O fool, hold fast to the Innate,
> And abandon the clinging bonds of existence.

Bring together in thought the restless waves of breath.
Then know the true nature of the Innate.
And this becomes still of itself.

After throwing:

    "One," go to Potāla (No. 60);

    "two," go to Tantra, Greater Accumulation (No. 42);

    "three," go to Shambhala (No. 59);

    "five," go to Wisdom-Holder of the Desire Gods (No. 67);

    "six," go to Tantra, Lesser Accumulation (No. 33).

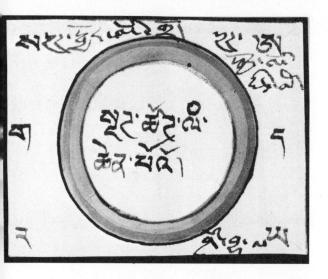

42

*Tantra, Greater Path
of Accumulation*

The yoga tantra is wholly internalized practice. The yogi creates mandalas and complex visualizations involving the Buddhas of the five tantric families. Generating the deity before one in all its detail, one's own nature is made resplendent by its radiance. Into this receptacle descends the real deity, called the "knowledge being" (jñāna-sattva). During the meditation one's own being becomes identical with the deity, which has been sealed with five seals. So "having purified all the conventionally true elements of existence and appearance into the state of mentality in the absolute truth (the truth of emptiness), one then generates the divine mandala with the five high Buddhas and seeks the attainment of causing the knowledge being to enter as summoned into oneself as the symbolic being (samaya-sattva)."

Four of the seals—the great seal, symbolic seal, dharma seal, and action seal—are applied with the appropriate visualization and hand gesture. "The fifth"—the knowledge seal—is being itself. They purify the body, mind, speech, and conduct, respectively, of the yogi. The term "seal" (mudrā) comes from the Sanskrit root meaning "joy"; it joyfully "seals" one's attainments (siddhi). So one is now without possibility of falling back into a lower path or unhappy destiny. Being completely identified with the body, speech, mind, and activities of the Buddhas, there can be no misuse of magical powers or slacking of spiritual progress on the bodhisattva path.

> In the practice of Mahāmudrā
> There is no room for thinking with a clinging mind.
> When realization of the State-Beyond-Playwords arises
> There is no need to chant or keep the rules.

After throwing:

"One," go to Tantra, Path of Application: "Heat" (No. 49);
"two," go to Tantra, Path of Application: "Climax" (No. 50);
"six," go to Shambhala (No. 59).

43

Independent Buddha
(Pratyeka-Buddha),
Path of Accumulation

One enters the vehicle of the solitary Buddha. This being attains enlightenment at a time when no Buddha abides in the world to teach the Dharma. He is described as having done attendance on previous Buddhas, but failed to attain liberation under their instruction. Being somewhat dull, not even the sufferings of a human existence nor the threat of death brought him to the point of Awakening. As a consequence of his practice, he was then born as a god with no further stimulus to practice. But steadfast in his revulsion from sàmsāra, and without hearing again the Dharma of the Buddhas, he continues accumulating merit by good conduct and solitary meditation, until at last the great Awakening is reached.

After throwing:
 "One," begin the Mahāyāna, Lesser Accumulation (No. 52);
 "two," go to Independent Buddha, Path of Application (No. 44);
 "three," go to the Heaven of the Thirty-three (No. 28);
 "four," begin the Vehicle of the Disciples (No. 38);
 "five," become a Nāga (No. 13);
 "six," go to Reviving Hell (No. 6).

Independent Buddha, Path of Application

When the Buddhas are not present, pratyekabuddhas appear in the world. Splendid in their silence, very powerful, coursing alone like the unicorn, they discipline their individual selves. . . .

For long ages one resides deep in the forest practicing meditation. One especially pursues the four applications of mindfulness: of the body, of feelings, of thoughts, and of dharmas. In this last meditation one considers the characteristics of all phenomena: They are impermanent, not pleasant, empty, and impersonal.

The Independent Buddha is likened to the unicorn, who shuns the herd to wander alone in the forest. He is a legendary figure in the ancient Indian tradition of the solitary yogi, a concept that the Buddhists never fully shared, for the Buddhist lives in a monastic or lay community and is much concerned with social relations. The Independent Buddha is cited as proof that the Dharma, the truth about reality, is timeless, for he has discovered and understood it while the Buddha was not about to preach in the world, and when there were no communities practicing the way.

> Lay down the rod for all beings,
> do no harm to any of them,
> consider their welfare with a friendly mind;
> course like the unicorn, alone.

After throwing:

"One," go to the Joyful Heaven (No. 30);
"two," go to Independent Buddha, Path of Cultivation (No. 46);
"three," go to Independent Buddha, Path of Vision (No. 45);
"four," go to the Northern Continent (No. 20);
"five," go to the Disciples, Path of Application (No. 39);
"six," go to the Heaven of the Four Great Kings (No. 27).

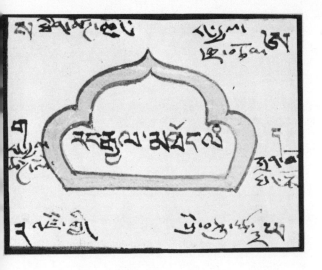

> Full happy are they for whom everything is indifferent; and
> they who dwell in caves enjoy the ascetic's comfort; and they
> who own nothing, and those who have no belongings, they
> walk the world lonely as a unicorn, they go like the wind in
> the sky.

Dwelling alone and far from the bustle of the world, the independent yogi turns his concentrated attention on the meaning of birth and death. He sees that sowing a thought, one reaps an action; sowing an action, one reaps a habit; sowing a habit, one reaps a destiny. In this way he discovers the laws of dependent origination. He sees that death arises in dependency on birth, birth on becoming or conception, this on grasping or copulation, this on sensation, this on sensory contact, this on the senses, the senses on the psychophysical organism, this on consciousness, consciousness on karmic conditions, and these, lastly, on ignorance. So he sees that if bewilderment is removed, karma will not be created nor consciousness arise, and so birth and death will be removed. He then is enabled to prevent the arising of defilements, for he has overcome the delusion that life is dependent on a single continuing self. With this purification of outlook he begins the practice of the noble eightfold path toward complete Awakening.

After throwing:

"One," begin the Mahāyāna, Lesser Accumulation (No. 52);
"two," go to Independent Buddha, Arhatship (No. 47);
"three," go to Independent Buddha, Cultivation (No. 46);
"four," go to Disciples, Paths of Vision and Cultivation (No. 40);
"five," go to the Southern Continent (No. 17);
"six," go to the Heaven of the Thirty-three (No. 28).

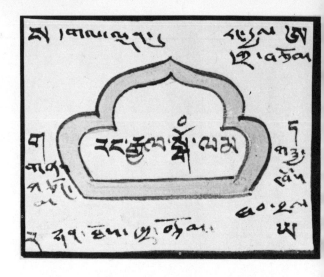

46

Independent Buddha, Path of Cultivation

By assiduous meditation on his vision of reality, the pratyeka-buddha destroys all attachment that can arise from grasping, rejecting, or bewildered relationship with the world. At his refined level of existence, all that remains is the attachment to *being* itself. Without a guide, by his own exertions, he comes to the verge of freedom from rebirth.

Because he is a self-made yogi, the powers of the Independent Buddha far exceed those of the disciple, who is timidly dependent on the instructions of others. The Independent Buddha is able to perform miracles, to divide his body and appear double, or to transform it into any shape; though in the habit of avoiding attachment to the external world in general and social entanglements in particular, if need be he will use his high awareness for the benefit of others, and give simple instructions as to the proper lifestyle of a yogi.

After throwing:

    "One," go to the Joyful Heaven (No. 30);
    "two," go to Independent Buddha, Arhatship (No. 47);
    "three," go to the Pure Abodes (No. 37);
    "four," go to the Realm of Form (No. 35);
    "five," go to Disciples, Arhatship (No. 51);
    "six," go to the Heaven Without Fighting (No. 29).

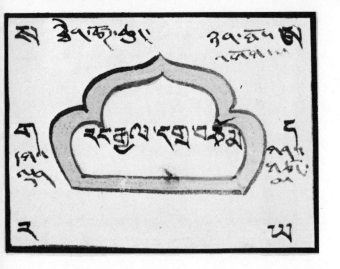

47

Independent Buddha, Arhatship

The solitary yogi attains an Awakened state. This is the "fifth path," called "no more study." He attains the nirvana in which a substrate of existence remains until the time of death. In terms of knowledge and miraculous abilities, the Independent Buddha has come further than the disciple. Yet, in the Tibetan view, he may still fall back to a lower state, for full Buddahood and omniscience have not yet been won.

Because of this arhat's solitary habits, he has neither the courage nor the ability to teach others the way to nirvana, and he cannot remember the form of the teachings he encountered so long before. In short, he is not a bodhisattva. His attainment is nonetheless substantial, and he is considered worthy of worship by the world, having transcended it.

After throwing:

    "One," begin the Mahāyāna, Lesser Accumulation (No. 52);
    "two," go to Cessation (No. 48);
    "three," go to the Joyful Heaven (No. 30);
    "four," go to the Pure Abodes (No. 37).

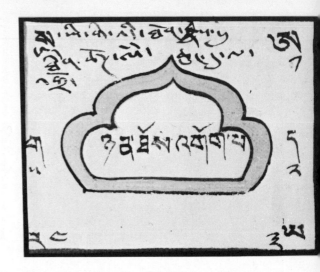

48

Cessation (Nirodha)

The Arhat has previously attained nirvana during his life, called the "nirvana with residue," for although all the defiling elements were eliminated, the physical and mental substrate remained. Now, at the time of death, he enters the "nirvana without residue." The nirvana with residue is likened to the elimination of all the outlaws in a saloon; the nirvana without residue would be the complete annihilation of the saloon.

Three concentrations are the gateways to nirvana. One understands that it is *empty,* for it has no relation to a "self"; it is *signless,* for it has no definition or determining characteristics; it is *wishless,* for it cannot be successfully desired. Nirvana as an entity is unlike most others (although it is likened to space), for it is independent and not impermanent; it is deathless, peaceful, and "fearless" or secure. It is the negation of the world, emancipation, the supreme reality and goal. "Like a fire, when the fuel is burned up, he is tranquil."

This nirvana is the goal of the disciples and the Independent Buddhas. Karma is eliminated, and the Arhat enters cessation. Sàmsāra has been escaped. Unfortunately, this is not the proper goal. This is termed "stationary nirvana"; it is opposed to the "nirvana in motion" of the bodhisattva. In the latter case, nirvana and sàmsāra are no different. One attains the great Awakening but remains in the saloon until everyone present there has also attained nirvana.

Lacking the compassion that motivates a bodhisattva, the Arhat in cessation can only be roused by a miracle. This is accomplished by the Buddha Amitābha, whose boundless light reaches even into this state. So roused by the Buddha Amitābha, one enters the Greater Vehicle.

After throwing:
"One" once,
"two" twice,
"three" thrice,
"four" four times,
"five" five times, and
"six" six times, begin the Mahāyāna, Lesser Accumulation (No. 52).

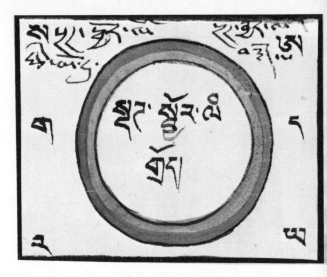

49

Tantra, Path of Application: "Heat"

Now the yogi, fully confirmed on the path to Awakening, takes the first great initiation or empowerment into the supreme (anuttara) tantra. With this permission from the lama, himself empowered by the previous teacher in the lineage, one is qualified to receive the transmission of particular texts, and instructions as to their practice. Four initiations in all will sow the seeds for the yogi's eventual transformation, through the stages of the tantric bodhisattva path, into the Buddhahood in its four forms.

The first empowerment is called "the flask"; it will grow into the Emanation body of the Buddha (top row of the board), Buddhahood in the range of temporality.

Before the initiatory sections of the ritual, the yogi is caused to enter the mandala and to take (or reaffirm) the vows common to Mahāyāna and tantra: the resolution to win enlightenment for the benefit of all. Then he makes the tantric pledges, the fourteen and eight basic vows as well as the particular commitments entailed by the tantric cycle into which he is being initiated. Even before entering the mandala, the disciple must be purified by previous practice and specific ceremonies. A special "flower garland" initiation is performed; one determines the Buddha family of the initiate by throwing a flower on the mandala and determining in which direction it falls.

The main part of the ritual is the flask initiation. The flask is filled with amṛta, nectar previously empowered by the deity and consisting of twenty-five substances compounded with water; this nectar purifies the body. If nonduality has not been attained by the flask initiation, one should contemplate at least that emptiness and bliss have been realized by the action.

> One should not think of molecules or atoms;
> It is this supreme bliss that pours forth unceasingly as existence.
> Error such as that is madness, says Saraha.
> Know but the pure and perfect state!
> He is at home, but she goes outside and looks.
> She sees her husband, but still asks the neighbors.

After throwing:
   "One," go to the Tantra, Path of Application: "Climax" (No. 50);
   "two," go to the Tantra, Path of Application: "Receptivity" (No. 57).

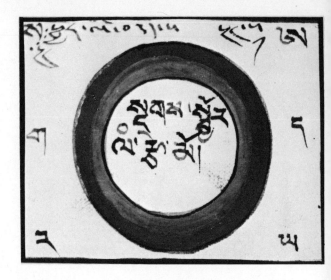

50

Tantra, Path of Application: "Climax"

One receives the "secret initiation" into the supreme tantra, which will bear fruit as the great Enjoyment body of the Buddha (No. 92). Here the initiating lama performs the activity, and the disciple is recipient of the benefits.

After drawing the deities of the mandala into his own body, the lama performs the "action seal" (karma-mudrā). He unites with wisdom (vidyā) in the form of a woman. The term "action seal" is a description of this yoga. The available text, written by a fifteenth-century Gelugpa monk, states:

> The "action" or "karma seal" is so called because by the karma of previous lives one has been cast onto the body of a woman and reaches attainment there. Whereas such actions as physical intercourse require no attention to meditation by oneself, but only the effectiveness of the actual seal, it is termed the "action seal."

When the semen, made molten by the fire of great passion, falls into the "lotus" of the "mother" and mixes with her red element, he achieves what is referred to as "the conventional mandala of the thought of enlightenment." The resultant mixture is tasted by the united "father-mother," and when it reaches the throat they can generate concretely a special bliss by which there is created in the disciple, who has been observing, an experience of the union of bliss and emptiness.

The author states that in his day a concrete vidyā is not used. Instead, the disciple of keen faculties employs a knowledge seal (jñāna-mudrā), meaning a mental action, through his own visualization of the union.

In either case, whether a concrete or imagined action is effected, the bodhicitta—the drop resulting from union of semen and menstrual blood —is transferred to the yogi, who is at this point in his career quite expert in the mental creation of events. This empowers his corresponding mystic veins and centers to accomplish the Buddha's function of speech. The term "secret initiation" comes from the tasting of the secret substance.

After throwing:
   "One," go to Tantra, Path of Application: "Receptivity" (No. 57);
   "two," go to the First Tantra Stage (No. 66).

51
Disciples, Arhatship

After many lifetimes of practice one has encountered the Teacher and by his instructions become enlightened. Thus one becomes a Buddhist saint, one who has "slain the enemies" (ari-han) of attachment, aversion, and bewilderment. One is worthy (arhat) of honor and reverence by human beings and by the gods. One is cool in danger, as the fragrant sandalwood to the ax. By spiritual understanding one has broken the eggshell of ignorance. The blue sky and the palm of one's hand are to one's mind the same.

The Arhat attains nirvana during his lifetime, but until death the body and mind remain as residues.

> Although there is suffering, no one is afflicted,
> No agent, but activity is a fact;
> Nirvana exists, but the nirvanized is not,
> There is a path but no one passing on it.

One has done what can be done by means of this vehicle.

After throwing:
   "One," begin the Mahāyāna, Lesser Accumulation (No. 52);
   "two," go to Cessation (No. 48);
   "three," go to Pure Abodes (No. 37).

52

Mahāyāna, Lesser Path of Accumulation

Beginning the Greater Vehicle, one conceives the intention of reaching enlightenment for the sake of all living beings. This is the "thought of awakening," bodhicitta, as yet only a vague intention, which will develop with practice into the enlightened mind.

"The Path of Accumulation is the morality of ordinary persons, the control of their senses, moderation in nourishment, watchfulness even during the early and later watches of the night, their energy, their calm and insight, their state of constant attention. It is also the merit acquired by other practices, the wisdom acquired by study, by reflection and by meditative cultivation (of what has been studied). By the development of these qualities one obtains receptivity to the comprehension (of the truth) and to liberation."

By practices of generosity, offerings, moral conduct, patience, vigor, and meditation one accumulates the merit that will bear fruit in the Enjoyment body of the Buddha. By the accumulation of study leading to wisdom one advances toward the attainment of the Dharma body.

In one's meditations one aims at gaining concentration of mind (samādhi) and the higher awarenesses (abhijñā) that will enable one to more effectively understand the doctrine and to help others. Basic to concentration is the state of calm (śamatha). Basic to calm are moral and devotional activities.

On this lower Path of Accumulation one turns one's constant attentions to the four objects of mindfulness—body, feelings, thoughts, and dharmas

—or to some other topic of meditation, either particular or abstract, that is appropriate to one's temperament. Bhavya says:

> The mind is a straying elephant:
> It is tied firmly to the strong post of Topic
> By the rope of Mindfulness:
> So for the mind: Compose it in Calm.

After throwing:

"One," go to Mahāyāna, Greater Path of Accumulation (No. 54);
"two," go to Mahāyāna, Middle Path of Accumulation (No. 53);
"three," go to the Joyful Heaven (No. 30);
"four," begin the Vehicle of the Disciples (No. 38);
"five," become an Animal (No. 11);
"six," go to the Cold Hells (No. 7).

53

Mahāyāna, Middle Path of Accumulation

Having fortified one's resolve to reach full Awakening and to lead all others there, one continues to gather the equipment of merit and understanding. The grosser distractions become stilled, and meditation rises to an intermediate level on the way to concentration.

One cultivates the five roots "conducive to liberation": *faith* in the Three Jewels, *vigor* in all practices, *mindfulness* of others, *concentration* free from discrimination between subject and object, and *wisdom* (the knowledge of dharmas and all their modifications). These gradually replace the five major obstacles to meditation: sense desire, ill will, laziness, agitation/guilt, and doubt.

One exerts oneself in the four right efforts: to prevent the arising of unwholesome mental states, to abandon those that exist, to produce wholesome mental states, and to nurture those that already exist.

At this stage, before the higher awarenesses have been obtained, one has only the intention of being useful to others, but one is able to do very little actual good. Therefore it is of little benefit to teach or converse about the Dharma. Atīśa emphasizes this point:

> Just as a bird with unfledged wings
> Cannot fly up into the sky,
> So a person who lacks the special knowledges
> Cannot work for the welfare of others.

And in an excursus on the foolishness of idle conversation, he says again:

> Like bending and wavering grass,
> That person is sure to have doubts. . . .
> For him the mind will never be sure!
> These are the faults of the person who likes to talk,

Like one who sits in a crowd watching a play,
And talks about the talents of another hero,
While his own attention worsens!
These are the faults of the person who likes to talk.

After throwing:

    "One," go to Mahāyāna, Path of Application: "Heat" (No. 55);
    "two," go to Mahāyāna, Greater Path of Accumulation (No. 54);
    "three," go to the Pure Abodes (No. 37);
    "four," go to Disciples, Paths of Vision and Cultivation (No. 40);
    "five," become an Asura (No. 15);
    "six," go to the Temporary Hells (No. 8).

54

Mahāyāna, Greater Path of Accumulation

Congratulations! You are irreversible! From this point you cannot fall back to a lower destiny. Several benefits accrue from the attainment of calm and concentration. First, one develops the four bases of psychic power. The first basis is endowed with concentration from desire-to-do combined with effort, which is based upon detachment, dispassion, and cessation (of discursive thinking), dedicated to self-surrender. The last three bases are endowed with concentration from vigor, thought, and examination, respectively.

Upon these bases one develops the higher awarenesses: the divine eye (to see all places in the universe), divine ear (to hear all sounds), knowledge of others' thoughts, knowledge of the past lives of oneself and others, and psychic powers. This last includes miraculous strength, radiation of light, transmutation of elements, and control over appearances (for example, the ability to create phantom bodies). These are considered prerequisites for preaching the Dharma.

In addition, one may enjoy the concentration called "following the flow of Dharma" (Dharma-srotānugata-samādhi), which enables one to travel to heavens and Buddha fields to audit the teachings of the various Buddhas and high bodhisattvas.

After throwing:
"One," go to Mahāyāna, Path of Application: "Receptivity" (No. 63);
"two," go to Mahāyāna, Path of Application: "Heat" (No. 55);
"three," go to Potāla (No. 60);
"four," go to Shambhala (No. 59).

55

Mahāyāna, Path of Application: "Heat" (Ūṣman)

Turning one's concentrated attention to the empty nature of reality, one develops the first of the "wholesome roots conducive to penetration," designated as "heat." This experience occurs also in the form of light, and the concentration characteristic of this stage is called "that which has obtained the light of the Dharma" (dharmāloka-labdha-samādhi). It is an examination of the doctrine so intensive that it generates heat and light, and the defilements burn away. In particular, one applies oneself to the idea that phenomena are not external realities but mental events and that their apparent characteristics are the result of discursive thought.

> This rebirth has arisen from discursive thought,
> Its very essence (ātman) is discursive thought;
> So to eliminate discursiveness completely,
> Is the very excellent nirvana.

"Application" in the title of this path refers to the application of one's meditative ability—the "calm" state of mind—to understanding the true nature of reality. In the Greater Vehicle, however, enlightenment is a function of compassion as well as of understanding. So the yoga of this stage is described also in terms of one's relations with others:

> . . . those on the stage of *Heat* make all beings into an object [of their thoughts]: their thoughts are described [first of all] as even [friendly, well-disposed, free from aversion, free from harm; and then] as tenfold [insofar as one regards all beings as if they were one's mother, father, brother, sister, son, daughter, friend, relative, kinsman, or maternal relative].

After throwing:

"One," go to Mahāyāna, Path of Application: "Receptivity" (No. 63);
"two," go to Mahāyāna, Path of Application: "Climax" (No. 56).

56

Mahāyāna,
Path of Application:
"Climax" (Mūrdhan)

One's exertions on the path of yoga, giving rise to experiences of heat and light, reach their peak. This is the second of four "roots of penetration," characterized by "the concentration that expands the light (of the Dharma)" (āloka-vṛddhi-samādhi). The duality of subject and object has disappeared, and one is established in the understanding of "thought only." Things are none other than reflections of mind. Even while dreaming, one looks upon all dharmas as a dream. At this stage the object of perception is destroyed. One understands the process of dependent origination in the Mahāyāna way: Not only is the living individual without an abiding principle or self, but so also are all phenomena "selfless," in that they originate in dependency on one another, and ultimately on the fabricating mind. Not only is one's own rebirth derived from the twelvefold chain, but so also is the existence of the whole world.

> Discursive thought is the great bewilderment,
> Casting us into the ocean of rebirth;
> Abiding in the nondiscursive concentration,
> One is clear in nonconception like the sky.

Here the physical and mental constituents of one's being have been replaced by the five cardinal virtues: faith, vigor, mindfulness, concentration, and wisdom. One has control over natural events, being able to prevent natural catastrophes, put out fires, and exorcise demons. Realizing that the world is made by mind, one is enabled to control and reform it in accord with one's noble intentions.

In terms of his relationships with others, the yogi is not only purified, generous, and moral himself, but able to teach others to be so as well.

After throwing:

"One," go to Mahāyāna, Path of Application: "Highest Teachings" (No. 64);

"two," go to Mahāyāna, Path of Application: "Receptivity" (No. 63).

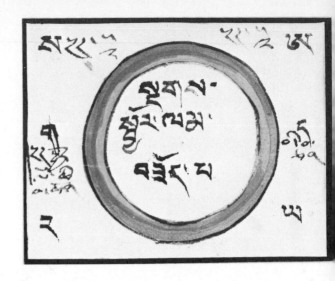

57

Tantra, Path of
Application: "Receptivity"

The yogi takes the third initiation, known as "wisdom-understanding" (prajñā-jñāna), into the supreme tantra. Here the lama, disciple, and wisdom lady (vidyā,) having "emerged from the experience of the common path as taught in the tantras" (see No. 50), and having blessed their streams of consciousness with mantras, accomplish the initiation of the disciple.

The initiation is given by a master fully qualified in such things as the "sixty arts of love" of the *kāma-śāstra* literature. Now the disciple unites with the wisdom lady. During union he draws breath down into the middle vein. As the "white element" descends from forehead to neck, he experiences "joy"; as it reaches the heart, "higher joy"; the navel, "special joy"; and reaching the tip of the thunderbolt gem, without being emitted, he realizes "spontaneous" or "co-emergent (saha-ja) bliss."

Preferably the union should be done by visualization, with a knowledge seal—an imagined partner—rather than an actual woman, for the yogi at this stage has powers of visualization that can make the imagined act more real and effective than one performed physically.

By the internal union of the two symbols into the "god of love," all duality comes to an end, and bliss-emptiness is achieved. The term "co-emergent" bliss is used because bliss and emptiness are not two entities to be merged. The mind that experiences bliss from yogic practice becomes simultaneously the mind that understands the truth of emptiness. Bliss and emptiness merge together, like the pouring of water into water.

Even if the bliss is not attained, the initiation implants seeds that, with later meditation on the Clear Light, will grow into the Buddha in his form as knowledge, the Dharma body, and the direct experience of emptiness.

> Once in the realm that's full of joy
> The seeing mind becomes enriched
> And thereby for this and that most useful;
>   even when it runs
> After objects it is not alienated from itself.
>
> The buds of joy and pleasure
> And the leaves of glory grow.
> If nothing flows out anywhere
> The bliss unspeakable will fruit.

After throwing:

"One," go to the First Tantra Stage (No. 66);

"two," go to the Second Tantra Stage (No. 73);

"three," go to Tantra, Path of Application: "Highest Teachings" (No. 58);

"four," go to the Land of Bliss (No. 77).

58
Tantra, Path of Application: "Highest Teachings"

The final initiation of the disciple is termed "the word," for here the guru explains to him how to understand the act of unification which was performed in the "wisdom-understanding" initiation. The guru says:

> During the third initiation, even if there was no concrete realization of the "father-mother god of love" (by means of the union) of your physical being with the vidyā, yet from the corresponding state of mental clarity, there was the simultaneous emergence of a blissful-empty mind with the symbolic Clear Light. Just so, in the course of (practicing) the path according to this, having cut through to the focal points (cakras) in the body, after meditative cultivation, at the higher limit of the fourth stage (of joy), the body will actually become the vajra-body (or) rainbow-body which was attained through the very subtle mind and through (the realization that reality is) mind only. In addition, your mind also became the Clear Light whose object is the direct under-

standing of emptiness. These having been combined, the attainment of the union of body and mind in that way is known as "union in (the process) of learning." By continuing to meditate along the same lines, one will attain the rank of the Buddha which is the "union beyond learning."

Such is the highest worldly dharma of the tantric path. Like the teachings of the equivalent Mahāyāna level it is still "worldly" because it has been learned on the level of instruction or initiation, and has yet to be realized in practice.

After throwing:

"One," go to the Second Tantra Stage (No. 73);
"two," go to Third Tantra Stage (No. 74);
"three," go to the First Tantra Stage (No. 66);
"four," go to the Realm of Superjoy (No. 85).

59

Shambhala

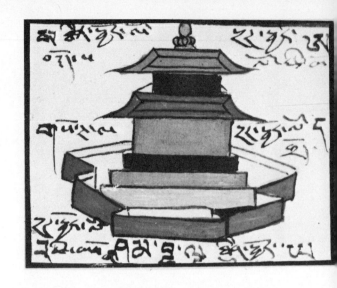

Ruled by a dynasty of tantric masters, Shambhala was originally converted by fierce bodhisattvas. The city sits by the Sita River (known also as the Tarim River in Central Asia), a stream so cold that it numbs the body. It is bordered by snowy mountains, and a thick forest lies between Shambhala and Tibet. The city is depicted in the shape of an eight-petaled lotus, and is crowded with wonderful buildings inhabited by tantric masters. At its center is the palace called Kalāpa, south of which is the mandala of the Kālacakra tantra, constructed with precious stones by the first King Sucandra. This monarch also compiled the first texts of this tantra, based on instruction by the Buddha.

The Kālacakra propounds a system of liberation based on astrology. Among tantras it is most heavily imbued with external magic, for Shambhala is continually threatened by the Turkish Muslims. The twenty-fifth King, named Ferocious Wheel (drag-po 'khor-lo), will in the year 2327 defeat these religious enemies in a Buddhist Armageddon. At one time there were hopes that this King was the Russian Czar. In any case, the battle is depicted in paintings of Shambhala.

For yogis Shambhala is, with Urgyan and Potāla, a source of inspiration, a mystic land of the Dharma that is not so far away as to be unattainable. One pilgrim, however, seeking the way to Shambhala through trackless wastes, encountered a cave-dwelling yogi who asked him, "Where are you going through these deserts of snow?"

"I want to see Shambhala," the pilgrim replied.

"Then don't go far; in your own heart is the kingdom of Shambhala."

After throwing:

"One," go to Mahāyāna, Path of Application: "Receptivity" (No. 63);

"two," go to Tantra, Path of Application: "Climax" (No. 50);

"three," go to Potāla (No. 60);

"four," go to Tantra, Path of Application: "Heat" (No. 49);

"five," go to Tantra, Greater Path of Accumulation (No. 42);

"six," go to Mahāyāna, Path of Application: "Heat" (No. 55).

60
Potāla

Visiting this island paradise off the South Indian coast, one encounters the high bodhisattvas Tārā and Avalokiteśvara. Besides the journey of the hero of the *Gaṇḍavyūha Sūtra,* there are records of several visits. The great pilgrim-scholar Hsüan Tsang described the dangerous passes and steep cliffs of the mountain retreat. On top, he said, is a lake whose waters are clear as a mirror. By it is the abode of Avalokiteśvara. From the lake flows a mighty river that circles the mountain twenty times on its way to the sea.

The people of the island on which the mountain is located have no special religion, yet they use magic to protect their homes. On the island are a number of smaller mountains with rock-crystal peaks and caves of diamond with high ceilings.

Geography is not the only barrier to Potāla; it seems that one's religious practice plays some role in gaining access. When the great philosopher-poet and grammarian Candragomin set sail from India, bound to the magic island, a huge sea nāga (the envious grammarian Patañjali) caused a great storm to threaten the ship. From within the sea he roared to the captain, "Throw out Candragomin." But Candragomin prayed to Lady Tārā, who arrived with an escort, all riding garuda birds, and frightened away the sea serpents.

In another tale, two yogis go there together. At the foot of the mountain, Tārā sits teaching some nāgas; but the yogis see only an old woman tending cows. On the side of the mountain she is teaching asuras and yakṣas; they see a girl tending goats and sheep. At the top they find nothing but a stone image of Avalokiteśvara. One yogi thinks, "This must be due to my faults of perception." Evoking the deities by meditation, he meets them and receives teachings. The other yogi meditates with little conviction and attains only the power of levitation. Even this he loses when on the way back he grows angry with his companion.

Avalokiteśvara and Tārā are the patron bodhisattvas of Tibet, the former embodied in the lineage of Dalai Lamas. Thus the mountain palace in Lhasa, which was their residence, is called the Potāla.

After throwing:

"One," go to Mahāyāna, Path of Application: "Highest Teachings" (No. 64);

"two," go to Mahāyāna, Path of Application: "Receptivity" (No. 63);

"three," go to Tantra, Greater Path of Accumulation (No. 42).

61

Urgyan (Uḍḍiyāna)

The magic land of the dakinis is located in the upper reaches of the modern Swat River Valley in Pakistan. A breeding ground for tantric Buddhism, it is identified especially with the supreme tantric cycle known as the Secret Assembly (guhya-samāja). This tantra has been promulgated as the path for those of strong passions and attachment to the world of sense.

> By the enjoyment of all sense desires,
> And gratification just as one pleases,
> By just such yoga as this,
> One may quickly gain Buddhahood.

This is twilight language, indicating in conventional terms the mystic transmutation effected by yogic practice. By such promises, couched in symbolism, the ignorant are attached to the Dharma.

The lake at Urgyan was at first inhabited by nāgas. They were converted by the bodhisattva Vajrapāṇi and given the tantras, written with lapis lazuli on leaves of gold. The nāgas became heroes and sky walkers (ḍākas and ḍākinīs, "warlocks and witches"), and built a city on the shores of the lake. The precious guru Padmasambhava was born in a lotus in that lake after the prayer of King Indrabhūti, who desired a son.

Urgyan and its Palace of Lotus Light was a popular pilgrimage site in the Middle Ages. The yogi known as Urgyan-pa has left an account of his visit there, during which he was instructed by the dākinī Vajra-yoginī in the form of a prostitute's daughter.

After throwing:
    "One," go to the Eighth Tantra Stage (No. 89);
    "two," go to the Supreme Heaven (No. 84);
    "three," go to the Seventh Tantra Stage (No. 83).

Hindu Wisdom-Holder
(Vidyādhara)

Having mastered the wisdom of the noble Brahmanical tradition, one's state is symbolized by the wish-granting jewel. One has grown powerful, a virtual lord of creation, at one with the great gods Brahma, Vishnu, or Shiva. The vidyā of which one is master is the knowledge of the Vedas, for all the Hindu practices, whether seeking welfare by sacrifice and burned offering, sun worship or devotionalism, dance, philosophy, logic, grammar, drugs, asceticism, yogic meditation, or merely keeping one's place in the caste system (karma yoga), seek their legitimacy in that timeless revelation. From the Buddhist point of view they are all related in their ignorance of the impermanent nature of all conditioned things, and their attempt to discover an abiding self in the individual and the world.

This tradition is one of great attainment. With wholesome action the devotee eradicates the grosser of the defilements, thus warranting the conquest of the wish-granting jewel. By strenuous meditation the yogi may rise through the trances to the very peak of existence. But for their attachment to the existence of certain entities—God and the soul—the Hindu is doomed to continued rebirth. There is only one means to complete freedom from attachment, and that is the understanding of the ultimate emptiness of all phenomena.

After throwing:

"One," begin the Mahāyāna, Lesser Accumulation (No. 52);
"two," begin the Vehicle of the Disciples (No. 38).

63

Mahāyāna, Path of Application: "Receptivity" (Kṣānti)

One approaches a direct and personal experience of the highest truths, firmly positioned in one's acceptance of the Four Noble Truths and one's commitment to the welfare of others. The yogi obtains the concentration that "enters partially into the meaning of reality (tattvārthaika-deśānupraveśa). Fortified by energy and concentration, he greatly enjoys consideration of the doctrine, in expectation that it will soon be fully understood. Each truth is realized first by acceptance, then by understanding. Here also the five cardinal virtues—faith, vigor, mindfulness, concentration, and wisdom—become unshakable forces in one's stream of being. One is receptive to the doctrine without the constraints posed by distractedness, doubt, and conceptualizing thought. This stage represents the dispersion of the "subject" side of the subject-object duality.

> Just as an elephant becomes gentle again after his rut,
> Mind rests in itself when its coming and going has stopped.
> Having understood it thus, what else do I need?

As a film projector creates the appearance of objects that do not really exist, so should one experience reality.

After throwing:

"One," go to the Realm of Superjoy (No. 85);

"two," go to Tantra, Greater Path of Accumulation (No. 42);

"three," go to Mahāyāna, Path of Application: "Highest Teachings" (No. 64);

"four," go to the Land of Bliss (No. 77).

64

Mahāyāna, Path of Application: "Highest Teachings" (Laukikāgra-Dharma)

One arrives at the stage of "unimpeded thought" (ānantarya-citta-samādhi). Immediately upon its release from subject-object dichotomizing, the mind rises to a direct and unhindered confrontation with the emptiness of all dharmas.

One now has all the equipment, plus the skill in its use, necessary for full Awakening. The stage of "coursing in faith" (adhimukti-caryā) is completed. One's own enlightenment is assured; ahead is the activity of the bodhisattva to alleviate the misery of others: skillful means conjoined with wisdom in the great mission.

After throwing:

"One," go to the First Sutra Stage (No. 71);
"two," go to Tantra, Path of Application: "Heat" (No. 49);
"five," go to the Land of Bliss (No. 77).

65

Wisdom-Holder of the Bön Tradition (*Bön Vidyādhara)

One has accomplished the way of the primeval Shen, the sorcerer of old who brought Bön doctrine to Tibet. The "wisdom" one holds is the companion with whom one attains Awakening. She is "youthful and well endowed like a tree of paradise. Her good qualities emerge everywhere like leaves and fruit and flowers, producing all the things that one desires." She is virtuous and compassionate, and above all difficult to find. In her "space and knowledge, Method and Wisdom, the channels, vital breath and vital fluid, all flow together." Grasping this perfect woman in ceremonial meditation one attains the *vidyā,* "original knowledge," by which creation was originally emanated from mind. One also obtains psychic skill (nyams-rtsal), the equivalent of Buddhist siddhi, which is "measureless like the sky," "unpredictable like a child's," "undirected like a madman's," "like a bold lion," and which "brings all conduct into accord with anything whatsoever."

In short, the Shen, the master of Bön, is a Taoist sage with tantric overlay, and this is the highest point of the non-Buddhist paths.

After throwing:

    "One," begin the Mahāyāna, Lesser Accumulation (No. 52);

    "two," begin the Vehicle of the Independent Buddhas (No. 43);

    "five," become an Asura (No. 15);

    "six," go to the Temporary Hells (No. 8).

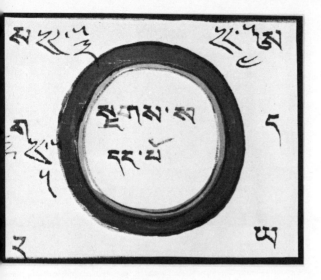

First Tantra Stage

Upon one is now conferred the first initiation of a vajra-master (vajrā-cārya). Having gone through the course of the tantras as a disciple, one will now be made qualified as a teacher. First is conferred the initiation by water, cleansing the remaining defilements of physical activity that obstruct the way to full Buddahood. One is enabled to see the Buddhas in many Buddha fields, to create emanation bodies for those who need instruction, and to convert living beings by the performance of miracles.

> To make offerings for the dead One needs qualities of the first stage; To emancipate the dead, magic power and attainment; to convert faithless men, the working of miracles.

The ten bodhisattva stages on the tantric path are likened to the process of death and rebirth. Previous to death, one accumulated the karma that will regulate the next life—in this case the taking of refuge in the faith, the bodhisattva vow, making offerings, moral conduct, study, and meditation. The moment of death is like those ritual meditations that brought one close to an understanding of emptiness: Death and the intermediate state (bardo, antarābhava) are like the Path of Application. Entering the womb is the mental generation of deity in the ritual meditation. The ten lunar months in the womb are the ten stages of the bodhisattva path. Birth from the womb is emergence into the full Awakening of Buddhahood. So one's previous practice on the paths of Accumulation and Application are the past karma giving rise to this supreme accomplishment, and the ten initiations are its maturation in the womb.

After throwing:
   "One," go to the Third Tantra Stage (No. 74);
   "two," go to the Fourth Tantra Stage (No. 75);
   "three," go to the Second Tantra Stage (No. 73).

67

Wisdom-Holder Among the Gods of Sense Desire (*Kāmadeva-Vidyādhara)

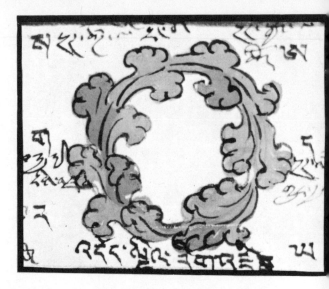

One becomes a vidyādhara equal in accomplishment (siddhi) with the gods of the Realm of Sense Desire. In addition to the ability to pacify, increase, subjugate, and destroy—the lower of the worldly siddhis—and the eight occult powers (listed at No. 72), one can also fly through the sky and make oneself invisible. One's body appears like that of a sixteen-year-old, and all one's desires appear from the sky.

The vidyā, simply speaking, is a female mantra. The holders of vidyā, "occult science," are known in Indian literature, Buddhist and non-Buddhist, from several centuries B.C. The vidyādharas live in cities in the snowy mountains north of India. They can fly and change shapes, and occasionally come down to intermarry with ordinary people. Tibetan historians consider them the original tantra masters among humanity; it is said the vidyādharas kept their wisdom secret until society had been prepared for its reception by the acceptance of the sutras of the Greater Vehicle. So the collection of tantras is called the "collection of the vidyādharas" (vidyādhara-piṭaka), to distinguish it from the "collection of the sutras" and that of the monastic discipline (vinaya-piṭaka). Nonetheless, in ancient times the sutra and vinaya masters were just as shy as were ordinary people of these "siddha gods" and their strange magic.

The forest of the vidyādharas is called "white cloud sounding everywhere the voice of the wandering mountain streams." They are described as "not quite peaceful and not quite wrathful . . . impressive, overpowering, majestic." Their monarch is a tantric Wheel-Turning King.

After throwing:
"One," go to Tantra, Middle Path of Accumulation (No. 41);
"two," go to Tantra, Greater Path of Accumulation (No. 42);
"three," go to the Wisdom-Holder of the Realm of Form (No. 68);
"four," become a Tantric Wheel-turning King (No. 69).

68

Wisdom-Holder of the Realm of Form (*Rūpa-Dhātu-Vidyādhara)

These radiant and powerful figures have mastered all the magic of the long-lived gods. Their abode is called the "Pure (land) of the Astronauts" (dag-pa mkha'-spyod). By mastering the vidyā spell they can prolong their life span for many ages. So subtle is the materiality of their forms that they enjoy all of space; they are astronauts who fly about the universe. Like the yogi in a high state of trance or the gods of the Realm of Form, they are aloof from the world and far beyond the enjoyment of objects of sense, which is gained from the lower siddhis by worldly vidyādharas. From the practice of tantric "yoga-without-images," dwelling in the sound of the mantra without specific visualization, they attain a state of pure calm and insight.

After throwing:

"One," go to Tantra, Greater Path of Accumulation (No. 42);
"two," go to Tantra, Path of Accumulation: "Heat" (No. 49);
"four," go to Shambhala (No. 59);
"six," go to Tantra, Middle Accumulation (No. 41).

69

Tantric Wheel-Turning King
(*Mantra-Cakravartin)

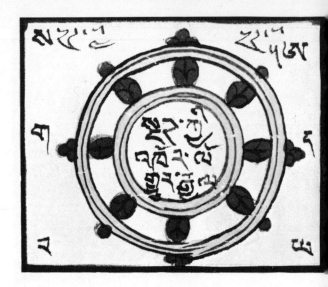

As emperor of the vidyādharas, one has attained the highest of worldly siddhis: universal sovereignty and recognition. This is the state of the ordinary Wheel-Turning King raised to a spiritual plane. Here the distinction between "path of graduation" and "path of study" ceases to be effective, for whatever is studied is immediately realized. The tantric Wheel-Turning King performs the activities of a great tantric scholar:

> In short, wherever he went, he used to read all available sacred texts, long or short. Everyday he used to expand the ocean of his Mind, completely filled with the games of knowledge. He became a great scholar similar to the *king of precious gems,* fulfilling the desires of all living beings, headed by those who possessed a strong wish for emancipation.

He combines doctrine and meditation in his teachings, and demonstrates the path in the example of his own attainments. With occult powers he converts those who have faith in demonstration of miracles.

After throwing:
   "One," go to the Fourth Tantra Stage (No. 75);
   "two," go to the Fifth Tantra Stage (No. 81).

Realm of Action-Completion
(*Karma-Paripūraṇa)

One visits the realm of Amoghasiddhi, "effective attainment," the northern Buddha field. This is the *karma* family of tantric practice. Activity is powerful, even destructive; its correspondence in unpurified life is jealousy; its prevailing color is green. But here the forces of passionate activity are turned toward effecting the destruction of hindrances and attaining the ends of Dharma. Action is precise, powerful, and complete.

Amoghasiddhi's element is wind. He holds a multicolored total vajra and makes the gesture of protection. His consort is Faithful Tārā, who guarantees one's tantric vows (samaya-tārā); the two ride on a garuda bird. Vajrapāṇi, "vajra-in-hand," is the bodhisattva of this realm; his function is appropriate compulsion.

After throwing:

"One," go to the Seventh Sutra Stage (No. 86);
"two," go to the Second Tantra Stage (No. 73);
"four," go to Mahākāla (No. 34);
"five," go to the Third Tantra Stage (No. 74);
"six," go to the First Sutra Stage (No. 71).

71

First Sutra Stage
(Bhūmi)

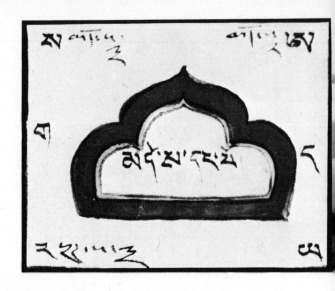

One enters the ten stages of the bodhisattva path, as elaborated in the sutras, the scriptures of the Greater Vehicle. At each stage the bodhisattva emphasizes one of the ten perfections of the path. Here he practices liberality, the perfection of which is the giving of instruction in the true Dharma.

"Rejoicing" (pramuditā) is the name given to the first level, for here the bodhisattva sees that enlightenment is not far distant, and with it the welfare of all. Like the purification of gold, his or her glory and value will gradually increase with progress through the stages.

"Rejoicing" is the bodhisattva's equivalent to the Path of Vision. Insight into the selflessness of personality and of dharmas provides a vision of the identity of self and others. There is no thought for oneself; he makes a great renunciation of worldly matters and is no longer distracted by the five common fears: concern for livelihood, reputation, death, future rebirth, and shyness at gatherings.

The bodhisattva makes a firm commitment to the thought of enlightenment and develops compassion for those caught in the cycle of rebirth.

He makes a set of aspirations: to revere the Buddhas, uphold the doctrine, emulate the events of the Buddha's life, accomplish the course of the bodhisattva, mature all living beings, perceive the extent of sàmsāra, purify and adorn Buddha realms, become precise and effective in all actions, and accomplish the great Awakening by demonstrating the deeds of the Buddha in his last existence (the top row of the board).

In preparing for this great mission the bodhisattva gathers spiritual and worldly knowledge. He practices the concentrations, the emanation of physical forms, and the performance of miracles. Like the leader of a caravan, he gathers provisions and solicits the advice of experienced travelers. Thus he also "rejoices" in mapping out the journey.

After throwing:
"One," go to the Third Sutra Stage (No. 79);
"two," go to the Second Sutra Stage (No. 80);
"three," go to the Third Tantra Stage (No. 74).

72

Wisdom-Holder of the Eight Siddhis

One has taken the path of siddhi, magical attainment, as opposed to that of study. By meditative ritual (sādhana) one practices the eight worldly attainments:

1. with the sword, invincibility;
2. with eye ointment, sight of the world from the heavens down;
3. with foot ointment, swiftness;
4. with magical pills, the ability to shape oneself in a tiny ball;
5. the elixir of youth;
6. the power of taking any form;
7. passing through barriers;
8. power over treasures and spirits under the earth.

These constitute the ordinary attainments; the extraordinary ability is, of course, Buddhahood, which requires meditation specifically on emptiness and not mere ritual service of divinity.

Some lamas consider these siddhi as equivalent to the Path of Accumulation. Others insist that one follow the orthodox tantric path.

After throwing:

"One," go to Wisdom-Holder Among the Desire Gods (No. 67);
"two," go to Tantra, Middle Path of Accumulation (No. 41);
"three," go to Tantra, Lesser Path of Accumulation (No. 33).

Second Tantra Stage

Rising to the second stage of the path to becoming a vajra master, one takes the initiation of the jewel-studded crown. This will bear fruit such as the head-bump (uṣṇīṣa) and other physical characteristics of the Buddha. One is thereby purified of physical karma, of misfortune, disease, deadening demons, and impediments to meditation. Indifferent to worldly gain and honor, yet filled with compassion, one is suited to become a universal ruler.

After throwing:

"One," go to the Fourth Tantra Stage (No. 75);
"two," go to the Fifth Tantra Stage (No. 81);
"six," become a Tantric Wheel-turning King (No. 69).

74

Third Tantra Stage

One receives the vajra initiation of a tantric master, which accomplishes the nondiscursive understanding that is characteristic of the Buddha's mind. One is freed from all traces of belief in an ego (ātman) and is more than a match for the rival teachers of other traditions.

> So long as you do not recognize the Supreme One in yourself,
> How should you gain this incomparable form?
> I have taught that when error ceases,
> You know yourself for what you are.

After throwing:

"One," go to the Fourth Tantra Stage (No. 75);
"two," go to the Fifth Tantra Stage (No. 81).

The initiation of the bell, female energy topped by a vajra, fulfills in one the ability to teach all the eighty-four thousand ways of practicing the Dharma, particular to all the types of living beings in all their situations. One is now authorized to perform the verbal functions of a Buddha and to have one's instructions regarded as those of the fully Awakened.

After throwing:
  "One," go to the Sixth Tantra Stage (No. 82);
  "two," go to the Seventh Tantra Stage (No. 83);
  "three," go to the Fifth Tantra Stage (No. 81).

Realm of Jeweled Peaks
(Ratna-Kūṭa)

The southern pure land is that created by Ratnasambhava, "source of jewels." He is the lord of the wish-granting gem, and fulfills the Buddha's function of giving what is needed. His steed is a horse, his color yellow, his element the earth, expansive and fertile. The understanding associated with this state is that of "equality," for all things are equal on the broad earth; it counteracts pride and cupidity. Ratnasambhava is embraced by Māmakī, who represents fertilizing water; his bodhisattvas are named Element of Space (ākāśa-garbha) and Wholly Benevolent (samanta-bhadra).

"One," go to the Fourth Sutra Stage (No. 78);
"two," go to the Third Tantra Stage (No. 74);
"three," go to the Second Tantra Stage (No. 73).

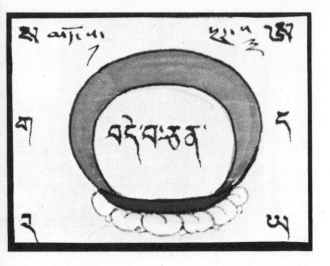

Land of Bliss (Sukhāvatī)

You have reached the pure land of Amitābha, "boundless light," the land of lotus ponds and magnificent palaces in which one's ordinary needs are fulfilled and one is able to hear while seated in a lotus, the teachings of Buddhas, at the merest wish.

The creation of this purified field is the result of a great vow made by the bodhisattva Dharmākara, "source of the Dharma," to create a pure space to which all creatures could attain. As Amitābha Buddha he descends to the believer at the time of death or, as the Tibetans prefer, projects a hook of light, which draws the person's consciousness—about the size of a seed—from his heart to dissolve in the heart of the Buddha and emanate from there to birth in a lotus flower.

Amitābha is an Emanation body; the corresponding Enjoyment body is Amitāyus, "infinite life"—propitiated for longevity; the Dharma body is Ananta-prabha, "boundless illumination." Amitābha sits in concentration holding a begging bowl in his lap, and may be taken to represent the Buddha's illumination under the bodhi tree. He is red; his family is the lotus and represents the transmutation of passion into compassion, for the beautiful, scented lotus has its roots in mud and slime. His understanding is termed "discriminative."

Amitābha's mount is the peacock, his consort the White-robed Lady pāṇḍara-vāsinī); the chief bodhisattvas of his family are Avalokiteśvara, the great compassionate lord who looks over Tibet, and Mahā-sthama-prāpta, "one attained to great strength." They are warm and open to everyone.

After throwing:

"One," go to the First Sutra Stage (No. 71);
"two," go to the Third Tantra Stage (No. 74).

78

Fourth Sutra Stage

At this stage, called "the Flaming" (arciṣ-matī), the various factors of enlightenment shine with great heat, burning off the remaining emotional and intellectual mist. The bodhisattva practices vigor in tandem with wisdom. He retreats to the forest and intensifies his meditation—examining the body, sensory organs, feelings, thoughts, and various phenomena of the inner and outer world. By ascetic warmth (tapas) he stills his desires and learns to be content with whatever exists. Nurturing a disgust for sense desires, he is purified by a stringent mode of life. There is no timidity nor faintheartedness in his practice. Nor is there attachment to the literary and artistic forms of the Dharma. As the noble Asaṅga puts it, " 'he has the conceit of having abolished Dharma,' inasmuch as he has abolished the conceit of there being varieties of Dharmas—'sutras' and so forth." He is nonpartisan and not opinionated. Yet he holds firmly to the middle way, rejecting the twin notions that everything is unreal and that everything truly exists. Both emotional and intellectual appropriation have thoroughly ceased.

Here the bodhisattva is like gold worked into an ornament. Intensive ascetic practices, combined with the wisdom of nonappropriation and the "middle way" between philosophic extremes, have perfected his moral conduct and attitude toward the world. Intensive meditation grants incredible supernatural powers, yet he is humble and pleasant to be with, mild and soft-spoken, splendid by nature, a shining example of his own teachings.

After throwing:

"One," go to the Sixth Sutra Stage (No. 87);

"two," go to the Fifth Sutra Stage (No. 88).

79

Third Sutra Stage

At the stage called "Illuminating" (prabhā-karī), the bodhisattva combines patience with the perfection of wisdom. That is to say, he will endure anything for the sake of the Dharma. He will walk through a thousand fires to hear the doctrine, and be patient enough to remain in sàmsāra to teach. Examining impermanence, he understands the suffering and burning of the world. He sees his own lives for ages past and the comings and goings of others. He sees how instruction in the Dharma shines from the Dharma-dhātu and resolves to use it to help others without any thought of reward. He truly lives the Dharma, day and night; he is elated by a well-turned phrase as though he had found a jewel. His life is total abandonment in service of the Dharma. His patience and gentleness with others are infinitely refined.

As the weight of gold is not diminished by its burning and purification, so the second-stage bodhisattva's moral qualities do not decrease, even though his specialty now is patience. His meditative attainments flourish. Lord of the Realm of Desire, he can grasp the sun and the moon or shake the earth, become one or many, appear and disappear, fly while seated cross-legged, walk on water, and blaze like fire.

After throwing:
   "One," go to the Fifth Sutra Stage (No. 88);
   "two," go to the Fourth Sutra Stage (No. 78).

80

Second Sutra Stage

On the "Immaculate" (vimalā) ground the bodhisattva is freed from all the stains of ethical violations. He perfects the practice of morality by combining it with wisdom. Thus he abstains from the ten unwholesome actions—killing, stealing, and so forth—and substitutes their opposites with a life-giving, generously compassionate attitude combined with the most skillful of means. Yet he also appreciates the Dharma-dhātu as the highest value.

The bodhisattva at this stage can produce a thousand concentrations, emanations, and miracles as others before, but now all in a single moment.

After throwing:

"One," go to the Fourth Sutra Stage (No. 78);
"two," go to the Third Sutra Stage (No. 79).

Fifth Tantra Stage

The yogi receives the initiation of permission (anujña), and the name he or she will bear upon reaching Buddhahood. The recipient is handed the bell and vajra—female and male, wisdom and means—the two tools of tantric practice. Thus he becomes a qualified teacher in his own right. Hereafter he is known by his initiation name. One has completed the "Path of Maturation" and is free to teach and confer initiations in accordance with one's vows and the rules surrounding transmission of the Dharma. All the qualities necessary for Buddhahood have been attained, and one enters upon the functions of the Buddha. The next bodhisattva stages are those of the "liberated path."

After throwing:

"One," go to the Seventh Tantra Stage (No. 83);
"two," go to the Eighth Tantra Stage (No. 89).

82

Sixth Tantra Stage

Having learned in previous stages to convert phenomenal existence into the forms of Buddhahood, one now brings to fulfillment, by intensive meditation, the four initiations of the supreme tantra. First one visualizes the deity in a rough and fine way. "Rough" refers to the limbs of the deity and "fine" to their placement on one's own body. The psychic winds are then roused to enter the central channel, and they dissolve therein. Concentration is centered in the heart focal point. When the heart knot is unraveled, the process of fulfillment will unfold itself.

> I have visited in my wanderings shrines and
> other places of pilgrimage,
> But I have not seen another shrine blissful
> like my own body.

After throwing:

"One," go to the Eighth Tantra Stage (No. 89);
"two," go to the Ninth Tantra Stage (No. 90).

The secret mind, which is equivalent to that of the Buddha in its understanding of emptiness, comes to experience bliss and emptiness in union. Guided by yoga in accord with previous initiations, it realizes a facsimile of the Clear Light. The process is known in three steps as "the light," "the spread of light," and "the culmination of light."

> It is pure and bright as a flower,
> It is like the feeling of staring
> Into the vast and empty sky,
> The awareness of Nothingness is limpid
>   and transparent, yet vivid.
> This Non-thought, this radiant and transparent
>   experience
> Is but the feeling of Dhyāna.
> With this good foundation
> One should further pray to the Three Precious Ones,
> And penetrate to Reality by deep thinking
>   and contemplation.
> He thus can tie the Non-ego Wisdom
> With the beneficial life-rope of deep Dhyāna

After throwing:

"One," go to the Supreme Heaven (No. 84);
"two," go to the Tenth Tantra Stage (No. 91).

84

Supreme Heaven
(Akaniṣṭha)

One has attained the highest place in the world and the most exalted Buddha field. Here in the Vajra-dhātu Palace sit tenth-stage bodhisattvas, great heroes who have attained the vajralike concentration. They are given final instruction by the Buddhas, who have the awesome form of the Enjoyment body (No. 92).

In this heaven dwell the highest gods of the Pure Abodes, surrounding and worshiping the Diamond-element Palace. Inside gather the Buddhas of all directions with their retinue of high bodhisattvas, whom they guide into the blissful-empty state of the supreme tantra. The aim of yogis on earth is to merge with these bodhisattvas and take the teachings as well, identifying themselves with the mysterious body, speech, and mind of the Buddhas by means of ritual gesture (mudrā), mantra, and concentration, respectively.

This realm is pictured in a lotus, the symbol of timeless purity.

After throwing:

"One," go to Dharma Body (No. 93).

172

Realm of Superjoy
(Abhirati)

One visits the eastern land of the Buddha Akṣobhya, the "unshakable one." Abhirati has been shown on earth by the great layman-bodhisattva Vimalakīrti, "Immaculate Fame," as one would show a wreath of flowers. Surrounded by mountains, this realm is filled with lovely lakes, hills and knolls, waterfalls, and ponds whose banks are sprinkled with gold dust. There are groves of gem trees, filled with singing birds and red flowers, which drop scented tissues and delicious foods. The inhabitants dwell in tents ornamented with precious articles; lotus flowers spring up at every step.

Akṣobhya is depicted in full lotus; he might be said to embody the Buddha's conquest of Māra under the bodhi tree (No. 100). Akṣobhya sits under his bodhi tree in Abhirati, "in the midst of an assembly vast as the sea, and preaches there the Dharma. When this pure land is thus brought to earth by Vimalakīrti, three precious ladders rise from it to the heaven of the Thirty-three; on these ladders, the gods of the Thirty-three descend to see, venerate, and serve the Buddha Akṣobhya and to hear the Dharma; on these ladders, the people of Jambu Island mount to the heaven of the Thirty-three to visit the gods."

Akṣobhya himself is imperturbable; he touches the earth to witness his conquest of the hindrances. His mount is the elephant; his color blue; his family that of the Vajra, more solid than anything else. The emotional equivalent (in the defiled state) is hatred, transmuted here into mirrorlike wisdom, "calm and uncritical," symbolized by the reflective quality of water. His consort is Buddha-locanā, "Eye of Awakening." The bodhi-sattva of this space is Vajrasattva, the "adamantine being," the tantric form of a bodhisattva.

After throwing:
    "One," go to the First Sutra Stage (No. 71);
    "two," go to the Second Tantra Stage (No. 73);
    "three," go to Jeweled Peaks (No. 76).

On this level, called "Far Reaching" (dūraṁgamā), the bodhisattva does immense works for the welfare of others. His perceptions and abilities are oceanic. He fulfills each of the perfections in each moment and in wide spaces of the universe. He creates pure fields in which living beings can thrive and develop their spiritual lives. He courses in his own practices and makes great strides in his knowledge of technique and supernatural powers.

The perfection of the Far Reaching stage is skill in means. The literary and artistic skills of Stage 5 now occur spontaneously and without thought or effort. He demonstrates the ways of the disciples and the independent Buddhas, as well as that of the bodhisattva, making no distinction of vehicles when it comes to the maturation of others. Now he is greater than the two lesser enlightened personages, the arhat and prateyekabuddha, in fact as well as intention. Previously his vow to effect the liberation of all beings placed him in the nobler class, much as a young prince is potentially more powerful than his mature ministers. Now that wisdom has been perfected, he is greater in his own right. He enters into nirvana and returns in every moment; while remaining within sàmsāra he experiences its transcendence. This is the "nirvana-in-motion," infinitely greater than the "Cessation" of the Lesser Vehicle (No. 48) because it continues to function in the world for the sake of the multitudes. Yet the bodhisattva strives for further greatness.

The seventh-stage bodhisattva resembles gold set with all manner of jewels, the most splendid of ornaments. Like the sun, he outshines all other luminary bodies, drying off the moisture of the defilements and maturing fields of grain that are sentient beings.

After throwing:
    "One," go to the Ninth Sutra Stage (No. 95);
    "two," go to the Eighth Sutra Stage (No. 96).

87

Sixth Sutra Stage

"Face to Face" (abhimukhī) with reality, the bodhisattva stands neither in sàmsāra nor in nirvana. He realizes that phenomena are neither pure nor impure in themselves; they can only be judged in relationship with others. He does not desire the peace of the Arhat or of the Independent Buddha, yet he is freed from rebirth. "When coming intentionally into birth he is protected there against the subtlest defilements (the saṁkleśas)." The basis of his life is not the defiled body-mind but the six perfections: generosity, moral conduct, patience, vigor, and meditation, all crowned by wisdom.

Wisdom perfects all the other practices of the bodhisattva; it is defined as understanding the principle of dependent origination. Observing the course of events, their arising and cessation, he notes that all worldly business arises from attachment to the self. Without this attachment there would be no ordinary and miserable existence. By that ignorant longing for being and/or nonbeing, people follow wrong paths of action; they plant the seeds of habit and inclination, which result in continued rebirth, followed inevitably by old age, sickness, misery, and death. Ignorance is the field for planting; the conceit that "I exist" is fertilizing moisture. So the sprout of the organism—body and mind—grows and develops sensory organs. As these meet each other there is contact, and thus perceptions, sensations, and the thirst for an impossible satisfaction. From that comes a clinging to existence; then rebirth; and from rebirth, suffering and death. He sees that the six destinies of living beings follow from ignorant activity. He understands that the world is mind only. Seeing further that this aggregate, or tree, of suffering grows without a real doer or experiencer, he reasons that no action can exist either in the absolute sense, for action requires an actor. Thus he meditates on the emptiness of all phenomena.

The sixth-stage bodhisattva glows like gold ornamented by beryl. As moonlight cools the body on a summer's night, his luster assuages the burning of those tormented by attachment and passion.

After throwing:

"One," go to the Eighth Sutra Stage (No. 96);
"two," go to the Seventh Sutra Stage (No. 86).

Fifth Sutra Stage

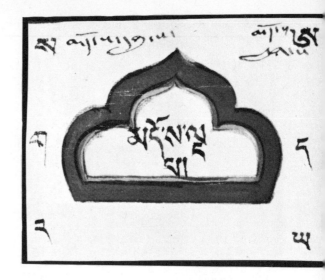

At this stage, "Very Difficult to Conquer" (sudurjayā), the bodhisattva accomplishes what is truly hard to do: He becomes a guide for living beings without becoming affected by their intractability. The characteristic perfection of this level is meditation. His memory is infallible, and so the Dharma-dhātu, the "principle of Dharma," is successfully reduced to the traditional formulations of truth. He can teach in terms of the Four Noble Truths—suffering, its cause, its cessation, and the path—and in terms of the two levels of truth, the relative and the absolute. He composes treatises on scripture, on the arts and sciences such as medicine and astrology that are conducive to human welfare; provides gardens and theatrical entertainments for the edification of others; and refutes the wrong views of less fruitful religious traditions. But he also knows the essential principle of reality, and for the fifth-stage bodhisattva there is no causality; the elements of reality are not seen as diverse but as being of the same nature, unoriginated, purified from the outset, free of mental conceptualization, beyond words, like a magic spell, a play, a dream, a reflection, or an echo.

The bodhisattva is now generally a monk or a nun; in associating with householders, he feels no envy of their situation or desire for gain. He is amazed at their lack of revulsion from sàmsāra and appalled at how they fuel the machines of continuing misery. He pities their bewilderment and confusion, but without arrogance or conceit, for he knows all streams of consciousness to be ultimately equal. He is skilled in showing them the Dharma as a guide.

The fifth-stage bodhisattva shines like purified gold adorned with semiprecious stones, or like the mansion of stars and planetary bodies that cannot be shaken off course by any wind. In short, he unites transcendental wisdom with the techniques of working in the world.

After throwing:

"One," go to the Ninth Sutra Stage (No. 95);
"two," go to the Sixth Sutra Stage (No. 87).

Eighth Tantra Stage

From the psychic winds and the understanding of "mind only" is produced the apparitional body, still impure because it is not immersed in the Clear Light and directly confronting the innate emptiness of mind.

> The impure illusory body of the womb-gate
> And the pure form of Buddha's body
> Are one in the great light of Bardo.
> Son, this is the *Bardo of Accomplishment!*

After throwing:

"One," go to the Supreme Heaven (No. 84);
"two," go to the Ninth Tantra Stage (No. 90).

90

Ninth Tantra Stage

The illusory body is purified by two trances: the contraction of winds in the heart, and their expansion into the Clear Light, which illumines the direct understanding of emptiness.

He entered the gate [of initiation] and began to contemplate, and he gained possession of a body of form which was "appearance and Emptiness." He was without outer or inner, above or below, front or rear, before or after; he was unmade, unlimited, undivided; he was without essence in appearance, without bias in Light, without defilement in Bliss; his glow was the Clear Light, his nature the unproduced, his prowess manifold. And in this realm of undefiled Great Bliss he saw the play—the residence and its residents, gods and goddesses, ḍākas and ḍākiṇīs—the subtle and self-sprung understanding, the miraculous knowledge. All events—inner and outer—were the appearance of his mind, occurring as the manifold process of his understanding.

From the moment he gained this appearance and Emptiness he penetrated it as the Clear Light, unconstrued, unfathomable, empty of arising, abiding, and perishing; he comprehended the natural pace of his ordinary knowledge as a genuine and innate nature, and whatever appeared as the play of the Dharma Body, Bliss and Emptiness, the pith of conditioned coproduction. . . .

In this state he purified away subject and object, and he perfected his prowess of great knowledge; as an attainment from this realm of the Clear Light of contemplation, from then on he knew that whatever occurred—at the very moment of its appearance—was itself light and itself clarity, unfathomable, unproduced, the nature of Great Bliss, self-sprung, self-erected.

He realized many "gateways to contemplation": the shining of gems, the lamp of gems, the shining of the moon, the lamp of the sun, the seeing of all things. There appeared in his mind endless insights, visions, supernormal powers, and signs of success, such that I cannot write them down, they were so many and so extraordinary.

After throwing:
   "One," go to the Supreme Heaven (No. 84);
   "two," go to the Tenth Tantra Stage (No. 91).

91

Tenth Tantra Stage

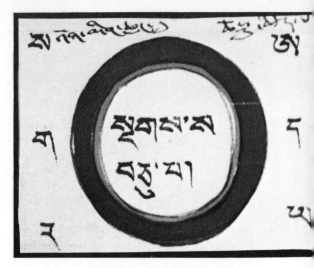

Contemplating the Clear Light whose substance is emptiness, one now achieves the real and well-learned unification (yuganaddha) of the body—the illusory, mind-made body—and the mind that is Clear Light. This is virtually the Enjoyment body of the Buddha, here experienced as a tenth-stage tantric bodhisattva. Just beyond this stage, rising beyond the world, is full Buddhahood, the unification beyond learning, the realm of the pure Dharma body. Yet the yogi, because he or she is impelled by compassion for others, remains in the world to manifest in the activities of a fully qualified vajra teacher.

> The fair tree of thought that knows no duality,
> Spreads through the triple world.
> It bears the flower and fruit of compassion,
> And its name is service of others.
>
> The fair tree of the Void abounds with flowers,
> Acts of compassion of many kinds,
> And fruit for others appearing spontaneously,
> For this joy has no actual thought of another.
>
> So the fair tree of the Void also lacks compassion,
> Without shoots or flowers or foliage,
> And whoever imagines them there, falls down,
> For branches there are none.
>
> The two trees spring from one seed,
> And for that reason there is but one fruit.
> And who thinks of them thus indistinguishable,
> Is released from Nirvana and Sàmsāra.

"One," go to the Supreme Heaven (No. 84);
"two," go to Dharma Body (No. 93).

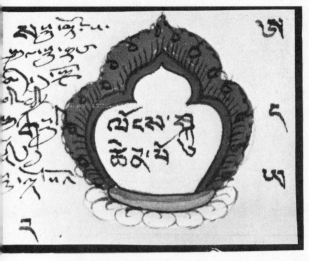

92

Great Enjoyment Body
(Sambhoga-Kāya)

Now one performs the functions of the Buddha on the highest level, initiating tenth-stage bodhisattva great-heroes into the highest levels of truth. This form of the Buddha is called the "communal" or "meeting" body (sku sprod-pa), for it is the sustaining power of the Buddhist community on its most purified stage, or the "enjoyment body," for it represents the fruit of the lengthy accumulation of merit and understanding. This body bears the thirty-two major and eighty minor marks of the Buddha: lines on his hands and feet depicting a wheel, golden skin, trunk like a lion, shoulders gently curved, hairs each curling clockwise, and so forth; it is depicted with ornaments of gold. In this form the Buddha teaches only the doctrines of the Greater Vehicle, sutras and tantras, and only in a purified field, the Supreme Heaven Akaniṣṭha. But like the sun and its rays, the enjoyment body radiates other forms, called emanation bodies, which are adapted to the ways of the world.

> The meeting body, in order to radiate countless Emanation
> bodies, meets the stage of the Emanation body.

After throwing:
  "One," go to Birth (No. 97).

93

Great Dharma Body
(Dharma-Kāya)

Like the sun, the Dharma body appears from behind the obscurations, produced from the path of Dharma. This is the great Awakening, the essence of Buddhahood. It is composed of the qualities of the Buddha, the powers and so forth, deriving from great compassion, and the two sorts of wisdom: absolute wisdom, which knows the emptiness of all phenomena—into which the bodhisattva has merged "like water poured into water, or oil dissolved into oil"—and relative knowledge, which is omniscience.

Yet these terms for the Dharma body and such attributes as "wisdom" are only descriptive, for it is beyond names; it is unborn and ineffable; it is not really produced, for it has always been all-pervading and needs only be realized. "One experiences the Dharma-kāya, joyful, equal to the sky, for only one instant: at the time of (1) death, (2) a faint, (3) going to sleep, (4) yawning, and (5) coitus."

The Dharma body does not exist, for its essence is as empty as that of all other dharmas; it does not nonexist, because this nature of emptiness is real. It is one, since the duality of "self" and "other" is a fiction; it is manifold, because many persons attain it, and relatively speaking, there are many Buddhas.

There is extant in Tibetan a "Praise of the Absolute" by the philosopher Nāgārjuna, and although he writes verse like a philosopher he captures in it the thought-transcending nature of Buddha in the form of the Dharma body:

However to praise you, Protector, unborn and without abode,
Quite surpassing mundane examples, beyond range of the spoken word?

Nonetheless, however that may be, though your range is the true Principle,
Let me place you in worldly terms, and praise you with great devotion.

With nature exempt from creation, you are wholly without birth;
Protector, you have no coming or going, to the nonexistent: All hail!

Neither nonexistent, nor real, neither continuing nor cut off,
Neither impermanent nor eternal, free from dualities: Hail!

Neither red nor green nor crimson, yellow nor black nor white,
No color imagined on you, to the uncolored: All hail!

Neither great nor small, neither long nor round,
Immeasureable being, to the measureless: All hail!

Neither near nor far, nor in the sky nor on earth,
Not in sàmsāra-nirvana, to the unabiding: All hail!

Shall I praise you with such praises or rather, what is such praise?
In the emptiness of all dharmas, who is the praiser? Who is praised?

How *can* I praise such a one, who has no middle or ends,
Who abandons both birth and destruction? there are no subject and object.

Praising the unmoving Well-gone One, beyond all coming and going,
By this merit may all the world, attain the Well-gone One's abode.

After throwing:
    "One," go to Enjoyment Body (No. 92).

94

Tenth Sutra Stage

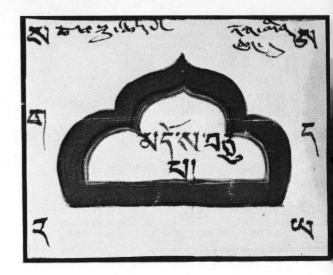

The bodhisattva has become a "cloud of Dharma" (Dharma-megha); his body is clothed with countless concentrations and magical formulas as the sky is filled with clouds. He lets fall a rain of Dharma to extinguish the glow of defilement still burning creatures below.

The practice here perfected is that of understanding, which means omniscience. All six higher awarenesses are his: divine eye, divine ear, mind reading, knowledge of former lives, psychic powers, and the knowledge that his passions are extinguished. From every pore of his skin emanate innumerable Buddhas, bodhisattvas, and so forth down to the least conspicuous teachers.

With rays of light the Buddhas initiate the tenth-stage bodhisattva into their own status, consecrating his sovereignty over the world. For now his practice of the high awarenesses and all his other actions pose no obstruction to his control over karma.

The tenth-stage bodhisattva is like a golden ornament made by a divine artisan for the king of the gods, studded with precious jewels and absolutely incomparable in splendor. So the great bodhisattvas of this stage are pictured with golden ornaments on their bodies: the compassionate Avalokiteśvara, savioress Tārā, learned Mañjuśrī, and benevolent Samantabhadra. The length of their course on the path is tremendous; all of this has taken three "countless ages," each comprising 10^{59} years. The first age reaches to the first bodhisattva stage, the second age through the seventh. Now these great heroes are fitted to assume the Dharma body, or to join the Buddha's retinue in the highest heaven.

After throwing:

  · "One," go to Dharma Body (No. 93);

  "two," go to the Supreme Heaven (No. 84).

Ninth Sutra Stage

This plane is called "right intellect" (sādhu-matī); one acquires the ability to teach the Dharma appropriate to all the aspects of a situation. The bodhisattva teaches like a Buddha. He or she can lecture on Dharma utilizing the four complete and specialized perspicacities (pratisaṁvid): knowledge of dharmas, meaning systems, etymology, and eloquence. He can speak in several languages and tones of voice simultaneously, making direct explanations suited to the various capacities of the members of his audience, and answer several questions at the same time. The perfection here is "power," but especially the ability to speak, including the power of the dhāraṇīs, which congeal the essence of the sutras and imbue their bearer with magical forces.

The bodhisattva's halo is like a golden ornament on the neck of a Wheel-turning King.

After throwing:

"One," go to Tenth Sutra Stage (No. 94);
"two," go to the Supreme Heaven (No. 84).

Eighth Sutra Stage

At the "unshakeable" (acalā) level, the bodhisattva ceases conscious striving for perfection. He enters the effortless state of the Dharma realm, no longer distinguishing states of mind that perceive the characteristics of things from those that perceive their sameness. He stands for no ideology, knowing that reality is beyond ideas, and enjoys the full acceptance of Emptiness with no distinction of "pure" and "impure," wholesome or unwholesome, among ideas and practices. His state is total equanimity. He takes no special worldly or spiritual form, not even that of a bodhisattva. Like a sleeping man who was dreaming that he had fallen into a river and was struggling to get out, and then awakes, the bodhisattva is suddenly relieved of all striving and anxiety.

In this situation the bodhisattva must be held to continued existence by outside influences. The Buddhas intervene to remind him of his vows. Even if the state of peace and liberation has been attained, he must continue to act for the benefit of others. The nonconceptual essence of Dharma, they point out to him, is permanent, whether people become fully Awakened to it or not; in fact, the Awakened state is attained by lesser beings, such as disciples and independent Buddhas. But only the full Buddhas, with their insight into the nature of things combined with worldly knowledge and skills, can work to effect the Awakening of others. They urge him to compare their own advanced development, their crowds of disciples, pure lands, and innumerable lights of Dharma, with his own single lamp of illumination. He must, they point out again, come to fulfill his vows by developing the qualities of a perfect Buddha. Finally, they confer upon him the prediction of his Buddhahood and its time and place.

So the eighth-stage bodhisattva develops the ten powers of the Buddha: those over length of life, state of mind, necessities, karma, manner of birth, creative imagination, the bodhisattva resolution, miracles, understanding, and Dharma discourse. He attains mastery over the realm that will become his Buddha field. This stage represents the fulfillment of his vows.

The bodhisattva's deeds are now thoughtless and spontaneous: they never fail. His dhāraṇī spells always protect. Indeed, all his deeds are like a magic spell. His methods are extended to embrace all the ways of teachings. Previous stages are likened to a boat going slowly overland toward the sea. Now he has entered the water and crosses vast distances quickly and easily, impelled by the wind of his resolution to save all living beings.

The eighth-stage bodhisattva is like an ornament of gold worn on the neck of a king. He approaches the omniscience of the Buddha, knowing all the intricacies of the world system, such as its size and age, down to each atomic particle within it. He appears in appropriate forms to the different classes of society. Like the sun and the moon in water, he is reflected in the affairs of the world, but without the slightest attachment on his part.

After throwing:
  "One," go to the Tenth Sutra Stage (No. 94);
  "two," go to the Ninth Sutra Stage (No. 95).

97

Adopting a Physical Form

By distributing emanation bodies in all the world systems of the universe, thus establishing the Dharma in the temporal world, the Buddha works without interruption for the welfare of living beings until the end of sàmsāra.

The emanated forms of Buddhas and bodhisattvas are known in Tibetan as tulku (sprul-sku, in Sanskrit nirmāṇa-kāya). When these are recognized among humanity, they are designated by the title rin-po-che, "very precious one." Most important for us, on Jambu Island, is the form taken by the Buddha as the "Sage of the Śākyas" (śākyamuni buddha), for he has established the Dharma and the Buddhist community on earth. One now performs the deeds of a Buddha, the great drama, as he showed them in middle India in the fifth century B.C.

Descending into the world system, the Emanation body takes the form of a tenth-stage bodhisattva, the crown prince of Buddhahood, abiding in Tuṣita heaven. When the time has come for human birth, he presents his crown to Maitreya, to the next Buddha in turn, and enters his mother's womb on Jambu Island. He has been advised by a divinity that in India the elephant would be the most suitable form for this descent. His mother, a queen of the Śākya tribe, dreams of this event (that an elephant entered her side), and ten lunar months later, while she is holding the branch of a Sāl tree in the garden of Lumbini, the bodhisattva emerges painlessly from

190

her side. He has the form of a man, born into a noble family, for such is the highest status in this time and place. There is no martyrdom in the last life of a fully Awakened one; he is lord of the world, master of his fate, with infinite skill and patience in dealing with obstacles.

The local gods, vedic in this case, have the honors of washing away the afterbirth. Astrologers differ as to his destiny; he has the physical characteristics—such as the inscribed wheel—of a Wheel-turning King, but some say he will leave worldly life and turn to religion. His mother, believing this and wishing to avoid the sorrow of her son leaving home, dies seven days after his birth and ascends to the heaven of the Thirty-three.

The bodhisattva has a happy childhood and youth with some spontaneous experience of meditative trances, but for the most part he excels in worldly studies. He marries a worthy woman after winning a contest of martial arts to prove to her father that, although pacifistic by nature, he has the skills of his heritage. Surrounded in the palace by a circle of women and the pleasures of a crown prince of the world, he truly lives at the peak of human existence.

After throwing:

"One" or "two," go to the Setting Forth (No. 98).

98

The Setting Forth
(Pravrajita)

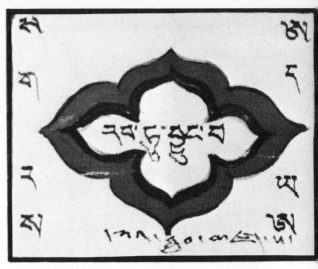

At the age of twenty-nine, the bodhisattva shows himself disgusted with palace life and leaves home to seek liberation from sàmsāra. The possibility of this departure has been announced by the seers, and his father, forewarned, has created obstacles to it, both physical and psychological. He permits his son no disagreeable experience, and blocks the palace gate at night with massive planks. But on some four occasions the young man, on taking the road toward his gardens, is confronted by visions sent by gods of the Pure Abodes. He sees an old man leaning painfully on a staff, a sick man, and a corpse being borne to cremation. Each time he is appalled to have his charioteer inform him that this is the general lot of human existence; each time he returns home to brood over the vision. On the fourth occasion he encounters a mendicant monk, calm and self-possessed, and is told of his disciplined life and his search for tranquillity. The bodhisattva resolves to follow this example.

The king, when approached for permission, offers his son anything he might desire. The bodhisattva requests perpetual youth, health, and immortality—or, failing these, that he may not be reborn. Unable to make a satisfactory answer, the king accedes to his request to leave home. Yet the king redoubles the guard and orders continuous entertainments for the prince. The songs and dancing make the young man feel like a caged bird. And when the women fall asleep, everyone in the palace having been lulled by the gods, he is shocked to see the ungraceful reality—"disheveled and disarrayed, breathing heavily, yawning and sprawling"—behind the sensual show. He looks in at his wife and son—born that very day—but is afraid to wake them to say good-bye. Indra, lord of the devas, opens the palace gate, and he rides forth on his horse in the company of the faithful charioteer. In the morning he sends them back, cuts off his long hair, and changes his silks for a hunter's russet robe.

After throwing:
    "One" or "two," go to Ascetic Practices (No. 99).

99

Ascetic Practices (Tapas)

In various forest retreats the bodhisattva encounters the foremost religious teachers of his day. He finds yogis practicing strange forms of painful meditation. Enquiring as to their purpose, he is told that they seek the purification of karma and a happier rebirth. This seems senseless to him, for the aim is not liberation. To the greatest saints even the highest bliss of the gods is full of the misery of impermanence.

He studies with two Brahmanical masters who teach the liberation of the Supreme Self from the body. But the distinction beween body and soul displeases him. A liberated soul is still an entity, and therefore subject to change and rebirth. The practices of these teachers leads to the formless states of trance, which he experiences and then rejects as insufficient. Joined by five ascetics, he makes his way to the bank of the Nairañjana, near Gaya, to remove false views with truly intense ascetic practice.

For six years the bodhisattva abides in the "space-pervading concentration," suspending his breath, slowing his vital functions, and feeding on a grain of rice or sesame each day. He sits immovably until the villagers think him dead. Finally his mother, from the heaven of the Thirty-three, begs him not to die without fulfilling his destiny. Perceiving that asceticism is not the way to liberation, he enters the village nearby and begs a bowl of milk and rice from a young cowgirl. His five companions abandon him in disgust. He washes himself in the river and advances to the great Sāl, the tree of Awakening, to sit in meditation.

After throwing:
   "One" or "two," advance to the Conquest of Māra (No. 100).

100

Conquest of Māra

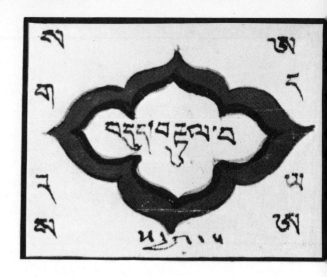

The bodhisattva overcomes the force and seductions of Māra, chief among all the gods of the Realm of Sense Desire. Approaching the Bodhi tree at dusk, the spirits of rain and wind freshen his path with dew and flowers. The mountains and trees bow in his direction; even newborn infants sleep with their faces pointed toward that tree, showing him the way. Taking his seat, the bodhisattva vows not to leave it until he has accomplished the great Awakening. The brahma gods, the devas, and many bodhisattvas approach to worship him.

At that time Māra comes to know that his authority is threatened, for here is one on the point of escaping the confines of his realm, and of showing the way to others. The word māra means "deadener"; he may be considered the personification of all sensory fears and distractions that obstruct success in meditation. Summoning his demonic hosts and mounting his great war chariot, Māra advances upon the tree, the center and navel of the earth. So terrible is his army that not one of the gods and devas dare to remain and face him.

First Māra takes the guise of a messenger and deceitfully informs the bodhisattva that a tyrant has taken over his father's kingdom, cast the king in prison, and abused the women. None, he says, dare oppose him, but all pray for the prince's return. The bodhisattva reflects upon the malice, lust, and cowardice reflected in such deeds, and determines to transcend the mediocre state of the human heart.

Failing in this device, Māra and his armies, in the forms of yakṣas and kumbhāṇḍas, rush to the attack. They cast showers of missiles at him, rocks and deadly weapons, but these all turn to flowers as they enter his aura, falling at his feet or hanging in the air as a canopy over his head.

194

Nor can whirlwinds and rainstorms move the bodhisattva, who is imperturbable.

Then Māra challenges the bodhisattva to reveal what merits he has gained to make him worthy of liberation. The great meditator admits the great sacrifice that Māra must have made, in past lives, to attain his state of the lord god of the Realm of Desire. Yet he himself has made many such sacrifices during his career as bodhisattva to ordinary creatures as well as gods, and furthermore with liberation, not power, as his aim. Māra claims that the evidence for his own sacrifice is unimpeachable, for the bodhisattva himself has just been witness to it, but that for the bodhisattva's sacrifice there is no witness at all. Then the bodhisattva, touching the earth with his right hand, calls the earth goddess to witness. The earth shakes six times. Showing half her body and folding her hands with reverence, the goddess rises half out of the earth to attest to his fitness for enlightenment. Māra and his hosts flee like smaller animals before the lion's roar.

Māra, however, has one more device. He sends down his daughters, named Desire, Pleasure, and Passion, to tempt the bodhisattva. They dance before him like the swaying branches of a young and leafy tree. They appeal to him with spring songs. Yet he is not moved by the image of transient pleasures. As the sun sets, his victory is complete. The tree nymphs come to praise him, while many of Māra's following are ashamed and converted, making the creative effort for enlightenment.

After throwing:
    "One" or "two," go to Buddhahood (No. 101).

101

Buddhahood

In the course of a night's meditations the bodhisattva attains the mystic illumination. Having subdued the various distractions presented by Māra, he ascends and descends, during the first watch of the night, through the four stages of trance. With his mind purified, calm, and freed from the workings of karma, he views with his wisdom eye all living beings. He sees them rising and falling on the wheel of life according to their karma. He sees the sufferings of the world.

During the second watch of the night he sees all the past lives of himself and others: the experience of the whole world. In the third and final watch he seeks the cause and cure for this mass of suffering. The results of his investigations are formulated in the Four Noble Truths: The round of rebirth is basically suffering, its causes thirst and ignorance; nirvana would be its transcendence, and there is a means to attain it.

Just before dawn he understands the nature and cause of suffering, this insight being codified in the twelvefold chain of dependent origination: Suffering and death arise dependent on birth, which arises dependent on reproduction, in turn dependent on grasping, desire, sensation, sensory contact, the six senses, the body-mind complex, consciousness, karmic impulses, and ignorance. He reviews them in reverse order: With the removal of ignorant activity, karma is not formed. Then consciousness will not arise, nor the body-mind complex, and on through rebirth and death. Wisdom arises instantaneously; he is fully Awakened and utters a song of triumph:

> Through many divers birth I passed
> Seeking in vain the builder of the house.

But O framer of houses, thou art found—
Never again shalt thou fashion a house for me!
Broken are all thy beams,
The king-post shattered!
My mind has passed into the stillness of Nirvana
The ending of desire has been attained at last!

For seven more weeks the Buddha subsists on the milkmaid's generous offering, she who is the first member of the Buddhist community. For the first week he sits contemplating the tree that was the site of his great attainment. In the second week he travels through three million world systems. In the third he sits again by the tree, and in the fourth he walks to the eastern and western seas. Māra tempts him then to enter final nirvana, giving up his body and life. In the fifth week a nāga king shields him from stormy weather, and in the sixth the Buddha goes to speak with some mendicants. At the end of the seventh week, sitting again by the tree, two merchants make him an offering of food; these are the first two Buddhist laymen. The Four Great Kings each offer a bowl to him with which to accept the food; he melts all four together so as not to disappoint any one of them. He sits again, intending to abide in silence and peace.

After throwing:
    "One" or "two," go to Turning the Wheel of Dharma (No. 102).

102

Turning the Wheel of Dharma

Out of compassion for others, the Buddha leaves his forest abode in order to teach the doctrine. At first, seated under the Bodhi tree on his vajra seat, he shows himself reluctant to teach what most will not understand. Then he is prayed to by Great Brahmā, lord of the gods of the Formless Realm, and by the chief of the thirty-three devas. He wonders whom to teach first. Knowing that his former teachers have recently passed away, he heads for Benares to meet his five former companions, although the tree nymphs warn him that Benares is sparsely populated and without shade. There he begs a meal and goes to the Deer Park northeast of town.

When the five ascetics see him coming, they note his unmortified appearance and conspire to treat him with disrespect. But at his closer approach they are overcome by his splendor and spontaneously do him honor —preparing a seat and so forth. He explains to them that he has not attained mere longevity, but has become a Buddha, fully Awakened and omniscient. These five become the first monks.

At midnight the Buddha speaks with them to create a rapport. In the last watch of the night he turns the wheel of Dharma. The "wheel" represents authority: The wheel of Dharma moves swiftly, sweeping all before it, subduing obstacles to spiritual development and fixing what is subdued, taking one to the far reaches of the world. "Turning the wheel" means communicating the Dharma.

In the first turning of the great spiritual wheel, at the Deer Park near Benares, the Buddha teaches the middle way between the pursuit of pleasure and self-mortification—that is, the Noble Eightfold Path. Then three times he explains the Four Noble Truths. The five monks reach the Path of Vision—understanding the Four Noble Truths—and from there they are quickly Awakened.

Among the eight parts of the Noble Eightfold Path, right views, intentions, effort, and mindfulness are said to be the four spokes of the wheel of Dharma. Right speech, conduct, and livelihood are the hub, and right concentration the rim.

In this first turning of the wheel of Dharma, aimed at an audience well prepared in self-control and meditation, but strongly attached to wrong views of the self and the path, the elements of reality (Dharmas) are held to really exist. The "self" composed of dharmas is said to be a fiction. These are the sutras of the lesser vehicle. Twice more during his last life the Buddha turns the wheel. The intermediate turning, at Vulture's Peak near the present Rajgir, teaches to advanced arhats and bodhisattvas the nonexistence of dharmas and the doctrine of their essential emptiness— that is, the Mādhyamika sutras of the Greater Vehicle. The last turning of the wheel occurs at Mount Malaya in the south and other places; it is the Yogācāra or mind-only doctrine and ascertains the nature of the absolute principle of emptiness. The sutras of the last turning show the elements of reality to be (1) imagined and nonexistent, (2) interdependent and "real" in a conventional sense, and (3) absolutely real in their nature of emptiness.

The tantras are included within the two later turnings of the wheel. They constitute practices revealed at various places but kept secret until much later.

In reality the Buddha never speaks a word from the time he becomes enlightened, for he has no discursive thought. Nonetheless, just as a hanging cymbal may be made to sound by the wind, without any gong to beat it, so his voice arises in response to the needs and dispositions of the various living beings who are his audience. From the Awakening of the Buddha streams the whole corpus of Buddhist doctrine, developed and elaborated over the course of centuries, which enables those who read it to eradicate false views and to attain Buddhahood.

After throwing:
    "One" or "two," go to Demonstration of Miracles (No. 103).

103

Demonstration of Miracles

To impress those for whom verbal teachings are insufficient, the Buddha performs miracles. Leaving the Deer Park, he returns to Magadha. In Śrāvastī he stays in a community of long-haired ascetics who are worshipers of fire. On the first evening the leader Kāśyapa warns him of a ferocious fire-breathing nāga in the hut that only he can handle. The Buddha enters the hut, and in the course of the night fights fire with fire, exhausting the wrath of the serpent as the ascetics, watching the smoke from outside, give him up as lost.

Then again during the winter the Buddha magically creates some five hundred charcoal burners for his hosts during a cold spell. On another occasion some baneful influence prevents them from cutting wood and lighting the fires for sacrifice, and the Buddha helps them with his magic. In the hot season a freak rainstorm causes a terrible flood around the hermitage. Kāśyapa, searching for his honored guest in a boat, finds that he has created dry land in the river.

In all, some thirty-five hundred miracles are required to convert this school of Brahmanical ascetics, who are not easily impressed. On several occasions the Buddha visits far-off points of the Meru world system, bringing back exotic foods: milk from the Western Continent, self-germinated rice from Kuru, the Jambu fruit from Mount Meru.

After converting the ascetics at last, the Buddha disappears for three weeks, vacationing in the heaven of the Thirty-three gods, where he instructs his mother in the Dharma. He descends again on a staircase of lapis lazuli built by the architect of the gods. One nun of his order, it is said, did him honor on his return by taking on the appearance of a Wheel-turning King.

After throwing:
    "One" or "two," go to Nirvana (No. 104).

104

Nirvana

In its final act, the Emanation body demonstrates the passing into nirvana. Māra visits the Buddha and argues that since the Buddha has completed his mission of establishing the doctrine and the community for this age, he should enter nirvana. Because the Buddha's close disciples fail to ask him to remain, he accedes to Māra's request. He cuts off the karmic forces supporting his life and lives for a final three months by psychic powers alone. Then on the road to Kushinagara, the site of his demise, he is entertained by a metalworker named Cunda, who serves a succulent dish of pork. The Buddha refuses to allow his companions to partake of it and has it interred after he has eaten. Later he falls ill with dysentery.

On the day of the parinirvana the Buddha washes in the river, and those about him marvel at his physical glow. The year is 486 B.C.; he is eighty years of age. Toward evening he lies down on his right side between two Sāl trees, hands under his head: the "lion's position." His last two personal disciples are encountered. The first, a musician, is converted by an appearance of the Buddha at his door, the phantom body playing a lute. The other, a Brahmanical ascetic, enters his dying presence and is persuaded to embark on the Noble Eightfold Path.

To his close disciples, too shy now to ask questions, the Buddha gives his last instructions on the doctrine and the community. He counsels them to accept only teachings that are authenticated by comparison with the Buddha's discourses, the monastic discipline, and the true nature of things. He gives instructions for the interment of his cremated remains, "like those of a Wheel-turning King," in a stupa built at a crossroads. Finally, regarding his passing, he makes his famous last statement: "Karmic composites are subject to the law of dissolution, coming and going they are impermanent; indeed, all phenomena that are born of causes and conditions are impermanent. Do not lament, but attain your goal without negligence, because by vigilance we come to full Awakening and the other fruits of the path."

The Buddha rises through the four stages of trance and the Realm of Form, and through the four equalizations of the Formless Realm. He attains the Peak of Existence, the equanimity of cessation. He descends through the eight stages and rises again through the four trances. From the top, a karmically neutral (avyākṛta) place, he enters nirvana. The earth shakes, stars fall, and rainbows and music fill all the quarters of space.

After throwing:

"One" or "two," pass your relics into the stupa above and become an object of reverence for the rest of the age—pervading the universe with your emanations.

Notes to the Commentaries

No. 1 Verse quoted from *The Hundred Thousand Songs of Milarepa,* tr. Garma C. C. Chang (New Hyde Park, N.Y.: Oriental Studies Foundation, University Books, 1962), p. 49.

Nos. 2–6 The Sanskrit names for the eight hot hells are, from the lowest, *avīci, pratāpana, tapana, mahāraurava, raurava, saṁghāta, kālasūtra,* and *samjīva.* Sources: the system of the "Sūtra on Mindfulness of the True Dharma," as in Matsunaga, op. cit., pp. 75–136; and Lin, op. cit., pp. 3–10. See also the system of Dhārmika Subhūti, in Mus., op. cit., pp. 218ff. Cf. also Gampopa, op. cit., pp. 57–60; "Le Sūtra des Causes et des Effets," ed. and tr. Robert Gauthiot and Paul Pelliot, *Mission Pelliot en Asie Centrale,* II. ii. 1 (Paris: Paul Geuthner, 1926), esp. pp. 15 and 18; AK, III. 148–55. On the Avīci Hell see G. P. Malalasekhera, ed., *Encyclopaedia of Buddhism* (Colombo: Government of Ceylon, 1956), under that heading. Verse on the Reviving Hell from Mus., op. cit., pp. 218–19. The term *avīci* is in the older sūtras only a description of over-population.

No. 7 The Cold Hells are found primarily in sources that derive from colder climates, not in the oldest scriptures. For their names see MHV, Nos. 4929–36. Cf. Lin., op. cit., pp. 10–14 and refs.; AK, III. 154; Gampopa, op. cit., pp. 60–61.

No. 8 *Prādeśik* Hells. AK, III. 155, and n. 1 on the name; Gampopa, pp. 61–62.

No. 9 TPS, pp. 582–83; Alex Wayman, "Studies in Yama and Māra," *Indo-Iranian Journal* III, pp. 44–73, 112–31; W. Y. Evans-Wentz, *The Tibetan Book of the Dead* (London: Oxford University Press, 1957), pp. 31–38, 147–48; Nebesky-Wojkowitz, op. cit., Ch. V; Alice Getty, *The*

Gods of Northern Buddhism (Oxford: Clarendon Press, 1928), p. 164;
Lin., op. cit., pp. 14–16, 18–19; Mus., op. cit., pp. 209–11, 243; S. Lévi,
Journal Asiatique (1928), pp. 204–7, 216. On Tibetan gods of hell see
G. Tucci, *Indo-Tibetica* III. i. Reale Academia d'Italia, Studi e Documenti
1 (Rome, 1935).

No. 10 Mus., op. cit., pp. 43, 249–57; Lin., op. cit., pp. 16–18.

No. 11 *Tiryak,* Mus., op. cit., pp. 244–47; Gampopa, op. cit., pp. 62–63.

No. 12 Mus., op. cit., pp. 163–64, 247, 259; Lin., op. cit., pp. 38–41, 61;
Hardy, op. cit., pp. 44–47. For a full list of such creatures, see MHV,
Nos. 3226ff.

No. 13 Mus., op. cit., pp. 164, 170–71, 247; Stephan Beyer, *The Cult of Tārā*
(Berkeley: University of California Press, 1973), pp. 295–96 with illustrations of peaceful and fierce nāgas; Nebesky-Wojkowitz, op. cit., pp.
290–91, 478 (a ceremony of rain-making).

No. 14 Mus., op. cit., p. 259; Nebesky-Wojkowitz, op. cit., pp. 14, 32, 35, 64,
205, 236, 280.

No. 15 Verse from Mus., op. cit., p. 283; cf. Lin., op. cit., pp. 24–29; Hardy,
op. cit., pp. 5, 47, 59.

No. 16 The story of Thar-nag comes from the biography of Padmasambhava
(Padma thang-yig), tr. Gustave-Charles Toussaint, *Le Dict de Padma,*
Bibliothèque de l'Institute des Hautes Études Chinoises, Librarie Ernest
Leroux (1933), Chant V–VI; related also by Tucci, TPS, p. 541. Cf.
C. Trungpa, *The Dawn of Tantra,* Clear Light Series (Berkeley, Calif.:
Shambhala, 1975), pp. 8–10; Francesca Fremantle and C. Trungpa, *The
Tibetan Book of the Dead* (Berkeley, Calif.: Clear Light Series, Sham-
bhala, 1965), p. 24–25. Thar-nag is one of a class of "proud ones"
(dregs-pa), and one of the "eighteen great proud tantra masters" (sngags-
bdag dregs-chen bco-brgyad)—Nebesky-Wojkowitz, op. cit., pp. 273,
281. On the four worldly siddhis see Wayman, *The Buddhist Tantras,*
pp. 76–77; Beyer, op. cit., pp. 249–50; Mkhas, op. cit., pp. 136–37n. On
Vajrapāṇi and Shiva see TPS, p. 218; Shiva and the asura, T. V. Wylie,
Nepal, op. cit., pp. 32–33. In *Tarantha's History of Buddhism in India*
(tr. Lama Chimpa and Alaka Chottopadhyaya [Simla: Indian Institute
of Advanced Study, 1970], p. 40) an old woman asks would-be worshipers of Shiva what austerities can possibly mean to one who allows his
mind to be disturbed by anger and cursing. Nonetheless, during the
course of Buddhist contacts with Shaivites in India, Shiva rises from a
demigod, chief of Yakṣas (Mus., op. cit., pp. 49, 55, 56), to the highest
of devas (MHV, No. 3108; *Daśabhūmika-sūtra,* cited Har Dayal, *The
Bodhisattva Doctrine in Buddhist Sanskrit Literature* [London: Routledge & Kegan Paul, 1932], p. 284).

No. 17 AK, III. 145ff.; AK, IV. 173–74, 223–24.

Nos. 18–19 AK, III. 146 and n. 1.; Mus., op. cit., pp. 144–47; Hanson, op. cit., p. 139. The shapes of these continents as painted here should be reversed. The name *videha* (Tibetan lus phags-po) is understood not as *vi-deha,* "bodiless," but as *virāj-deha,* "noble-bodied."

No. 20 Uttera-Kuru. The name *kuru* is translated by the Tibetans as "dissonant sound" (sgra mi-snyan), as though from the Sanskrit *ku-ruta.* The Tibetan translators are notorious literalists at times in seeking a Sanskrit etymology. But the sense of "dissonant sound" is not appropriate to descriptions of the continent. In fact Kuru, like Videha and Godānīya, derives from the name of a tribe of ancient India, and need not be given a literal Sanskrit meaning. Lin., op. cit., pp. 139, 145. Mus., op. cit., pp. 142–43; AK, II. 200; III. 176; IV. 127, 182; VI. 152, 174; Tsong-kha-pa, *Lam-rim chung-ba,* p. 60; *Dictionary of Pāli Proper Names,* ed. G. P. Malalasekera, repr. PTS (London: Luzac & Co., 1960), II, pp. 355–56. Compare Hardy, op. cit., pp. 14–15. On sandalwood from Kuru, see also Tāranātha, op. cit., p. 223n.

No. 21 Sanskrit *mleccha,* Tibetan *kla-klo.* Like the Greek *barbaros,* these terms refer to peoples of rough and unintelligible speech. TPS, p. 212; Wylie, *Geography of Tibet,* pp. 61 and note 93, 107. The origin of Mohammedanism is discussed by Tāranātha, op. cit., pp. 117–19.

No. 22 See note to No. 62.

No. 23 On Bön history and doctrines see Li An-che, "Bon," *Southwestern Journal of Anthropology,* Vol. 4 (1948), pp. 31–42; Gzer-myig tr. A. H. Helmut Hoffmann; *The Religions of Tibet,* tr. Edward Fitzgerald (London: Allen & Unwin, Ltd., 1961), Ch. I, V; David L. Snellgrove, *The Nine Ways of Bön* (London: Oxford University Press, 1967); Samten G. Karmay, *The Treasury of Good Sayings* (London: Oxford University Press, 1972).

No. 24 On the six colors, and those of the saviors for each destiny, see Govinda, op. cit., pp. 247–52, from the "book of the dead." For this latter text, and the process of death and rebirth, see the translations of Fremantle-Trungpa and Evans-Wentz, op. cit. Verse translated from Śāntideva, *Bodhicaryāvatāra,* I, 4.

No. 25 For a detailed description of the preliminary practices see the treatise of 'Jam-mgnon, tr. Hanson, op. cit. Cf. the summary by Beyer, op. cit., pp. 25ff., 434–42; and by John Blofeld, *The Tantric Mysticism of Tibet* (New York: E. P. Dutton & Co., 1970), II, i and ii. On the importance of the thought of enlightenment and making offerings according to Tsong-kha-pa, see H. V. Guenther, *Tibetan Buddhism Without Mystification* (Leiden: E. J. Brill, 1966), pp. 111, 124, 138. On tantric vows see Mkhas, op. cit., p. 328n; JA, 1929, p. 267 (the "original version" of Aśvaghoṣa); Guenther, *Mystification,* p. 100; Geshe Wangyal, *The Door of Liberation* (New York: Maurice Girodias Associates, 1973), p. 287; Janice Dean Willis, *The Diamond Light* (New York: Simon & Schuster, 1972), pp. 100–6; Beyer, op. cit., pp. 403–7.

No. 26 AK, II. 181, 220; III. 56, 196ff., 206 (on the Cakravartin dynasty); IV. 137–38 (on meritorious activity); Śāntideva *Śikṣā-samuccaya: A Compendium of Buddhist Doctrine* (abbrev. *Śikṣā.*), tr. Cecil Bendall and W. H. D. Rouse (repr. Delhi: Motilal Banarsidass, 1971), p. 171. On the precious articles see Hanson, op. cit., pp. 140–42 and illus.; Lin., op. cit., pp. 253–57; cf. also ibid., pp. 142–44; TPS, pp. 295, 306, 319–20 (on the Cakravartin's capital). On Aśoka see Lamotte, op. cit., pp. 244–83.

No. 27 Getty, op. cit., pp. 166–68; McGovern, op. cit., p. 65; Mus., op. cit., pp. 144–47, 283; *Dictionary of Pāli Proper Names,* I, pp. 861–62; Lin., op. cit., pp. 29–32, 55 (on the sexuality of the gods). On the sex life of the gods in a tantric context see Mkhas, op. cit., pp. 168–69 and n. On the temple iconography of the Four Great Kings, see F. Lessing, *Yung-ho-kung,* The Sino-Swedish Expedition Publication ⚡18 (Stockholm, 1942), pp. 38–52. On Vaiśravaṇa see TPS, pp. 571–78.

No. 28 McGovern, pp. 65–66; Śāntideva, *Śikṣā,* op. cit., p. 270; Mus., op. cit., p. 285; AK, III. 161–63, 164; *Dictionary of Pāli,* op. cit., II, pp. 1,002–4; Gampopa, op. cit., p. 68; Lin., op. cit., pp. 33–37, 55–57, 91–92 (including a different list of the signs for the falls of a god). The "thirty-three" is considered to refer to that number of places, not the thirty-three vedic gods. The places are named in Lin, op. cit., II, p. 14, n. 7.

No. 29 Mus., op. cit., p. 287; Mahāvastu, tr. J. J. Jones, SBE, Vols. 16, 18, 19 (London: Luzac & Co., 1949–56), I. 169; II. 327; Lin., op. cit., pp. 21–22, 54–55, 61–62. These *Yāma* gods are not to be confused with Yama, lord of the dead (No. 9), although in the Vedas he has also the role of a god of light. Both come from the root *yam,* "control," but these are taken in different senses. The Yāma gods are "self-controlled" (Tibetan *'thab-bral,* "without fighting"), whereas Yama (Tibetan *gshin-rje,* "lord of the dead") is the controller of the destinies of others.

No. 30 Verse from Mus., op. cit., pp. 286–87. Description of Tuṣita by the Fourth Karma-pa (the first lama rebirth to be recognized in Tibet), BA, 496–97. On Asaṅga's journey to Tuṣita see Buston, op. cit., II, p. 139. Picture of Maitreya and iconography see Evans-Wentz, *Liberation,* xxvii; Getty, op. cit., pp. 21–24. On Tuṣita see *Dictionary of Pāli,* II, pp. 1,033–34. Lin., op. cit., p. 62, describes a bodhisattva, king of birds in

Tuṣita. This is not Maitreya, nor is the King of Tuṣita, named Saṁtuṣita, as indicates Vimalakīrti, op. cit., p. 189.

No. 31 Verse from Mus., op. cit., p. 288. Other sources: AK, III. 164, 166; B. C. Law, *Heaven and Hell in Buddhist Perspective* (repr. Varanasi, 1973), pp. 88–89; McGovern, op. cit., p. 66. The system of divine levels of sexual abstraction in Lin., op. cit., p. 55, differs from that of the AK used here.

No. 32 AK, 164, 166; Lin., op. cit., pp. 20–23 (on Māra and his place); verse from Mus., op. cit., p. 288; *Dictionary of Pāli,* II, p. 153; Lamotte, op. cit., p. 761; Lamotte, *Le Traité de la Grande Vertu de Sagesse,* Bibliothèque du Museon, Vol. 18 (Louvain: Institute Orientaliste, Publications Universitaires, 1949), p. 340.

No. 33 Verse from Milarepa, op. cit., p. 271. Beyer, op. cit., deals especially with Tārā ritual of the activity tantra in its functions of worship, practice, and worldly siddhi. Also, compare Mkhas, op. cit., sections on Kriya-tantra, esp. pp. 163ff., against the Rnying-ma view of "god in front" vs. "self as god"; for beginners Mkhas admits the gradation of the Old School. For the Gelugpa classification, see also Mkhas, op. cit., p. 219; Wayman, op. cit., p. 53; Dalai Lama XIV, op. cit., p. 87; Geshe Wang-yal, op. cit., pp. 257, 283ff. For the Rnying-ma view see Blofeld, op. cit., pp. 220–21; Guenther-Trungpa, *The Dawn of Tantra,* pp. 2–3 (Guenther); Sum-pa Mkhan-po, *Dpag-bsam ljon-bzang,* ed. S. C. Das (Calcutta: Presidency Jail Press, 1908), pp. 389–90. For other warnings against harmful pūjas and Vajra Hell see Mkhas, op. cit., pp. 329–31.

No. 34 Nebesky-Wojkowitz, op. cit., p. 23, Ch. III, pp. 488–90 (the ritual of killing, without the text); TPS, pp. 584–86; Trungpa, *Visual Dharma,* pp. 22, 112; Beyer, op. cit., pp. 47ff.; Fremantle-Trungpa, op. cit., p. x; on the dances see Stein, op. cit., pp. 89–90

No. 35 On "immovable" karma see *Vijñaptimātratāsiddhi: La Siddhi de Hiuan-Tsang* (abbrev. *Siddhi*), tr. Louis de La Vallée Poussin (Paris: Paul Geuthner, 1928), pp. 474, 494. On the stages of meditation compare Dalai Lama XIV, op. cit., pp. 53–69 with Gampopa, op. cit., p. 80. On the gods of form (whose characteristics do not precisely correspond to those of the yogis in trance who are so reborn—AK, III. 162ff.), see AK, II. 129ff.; III. 2ff., 17, 165ff.; IV. 105; VIII. 180–82; Lamotte, op. cit., p. 761. On the "Thoughtless" stage AK, II. 199–200; III. 21. Only ordinary people (not Buddhists) are reborn in the Brahma realms, AK, VI. 214. For a summary of the three realms according to the AK see Lamotte, *Histoire,* p. 35.

No. 36 This square should perhaps come after the following one, Pure Abodes, for the latter is part of the Realm of Form. But here the potentialities for spiritual advancement are inferior, for one is too far out of the world for the path to be practiced. The higher awareness (abhijñā) may be found here, but not in the Formless Realm (AK, VII. 101–5. The descriptions translated from MHV, Nos. 1492–94 (in the first read *thogs-pa'i* for *thog-ma'i*). See also AK, III. 4–6, 15, n. 1; VIII. 143–44. For a refutation of the view that this realm must contain material elements, see AK, VIII. 135–43. On the "nonideation" equalization (asaṁjñi-samāpatti) see AK, II. 48; III. 31. Cf. Gampopa, op. cit., pp. 10–11, 80–81; Dalai Lama XIV, op. cit., p. 69.

No. 37 AK, III. 2, 168; IV. 213–14; VII. 103. Description quoted from J. J. Jones, op. cit., I, p. 28. On the five cardinal virtues see E. Conze, *Buddhist Thought in India,* (repr. Ann Arbor: University of Michigan Press, 1967), I. 4. Pictured is the characteristic flower of this realm itself called the "Pure Abode"—Dezhung Rinpoche.

No. 38 On the meditations for each type of personality see Edward Conze, *Buddhist Meditation* (London: George Allen & Unwin, Ltd., 1956), p. 15. For summaries of the five paths see Lamotte, *Histoire,* pp. 679–86; Dalai Lama XIV, op. cit., pp. 77–82; Conze, *Buddhist Thought,* op. cit., pp. 175–77; AK Introd. to Ch. VI, pp. iv–xi.

No. 39 Ibid.

No. 40 In a rather negative commentary on the state of the "Lesser Vehicle" schools, this path leads not to arhatship but to one of the heavenly realms. For statements of the Four Truths see E. Conze, *Buddhism: Its Essence and Development* (repr. New York: Harper Torchbooks, 1959), p. 43; Mkhas, op. cit., p. 43. On their sixteen aspects see Conze, *Meditation,* op. cit., Ch. IV; Lamotte, *Histoire,* pp. 681–82.

No. 41 On *ubhaya* tantra see Sumpa, loc. cit.; Dalai Lama XIV, op. cit., p. 127; Mkhas, op. cit., p. 100, n. 1; Stein, op. cit., p. 169 (this last misreads it as *upāya,* tantra "of skill in means"). On magical attainments in the Pāli tradition see, e.g., Buddhaghosa, op. cit., p. 183; "the water kasina is the basis for such powers as diving in and out of the earth, causing rainstorms, creating rivers and seas, making the earth and rocks and palaces shake." Quote from "Saraha's Treasury of Songs (dohā-kośa), tr. D. Snellgrove in E. Conze, et al., *Buddhist Texts Through the Ages* (repr. New York: Harper & Row, 1964), pp. 224–39, v. 44–45.

No. 42 Mkhas, Ch. VI; Beyer, pp. 100ff.; description from Sumpa, p. 389; verse from Milarepa, op. cit., p. 457.

No. 43 *Khuddakanikāya,* Vol. 3, ed. Bhikkhu J. Kashyap, Nālandā Mahāvihāra (Bihar, 1960), vi, 9ff.; Kātyāyana, *Peṭakopadesa,* tr. Bhikkhu Ñāṇamoli, as *The Piṭaka-disclosure,* PTS Translation Series No. 35 (London: Luzac & Co., 1964), pp. 1,012–22, esp. p. 1,015.

No. 44 Verse from the Pāli *Khuddakanikāya* III, op. cit., Ch. VI, v. 10. Prose paragraph from the Sanskrit *Mahāvastu,* ed. with Bengali, tr. by R. Basak (Calcutta: University Sanskrit College, 1963), p. 385. The English translator mistakes the first line quite unforgivably, writing "Whenever Buddhas, appear in the world, pratyekabuddhas also appear"—J. J. Jones, op. cit., I, p. 249 (buddhānām anutpāde pratyekabuddhā loke utpadyanti).

No. 45 Quoted paragraph adapted from Śāntideva, *Sikṣa.* tr. Bendall, op. cit., p. 189 (himself quoting the *Samādhirājasūtra*).

No. 46 *Laṅkāvatāra-sūtra,* tr. D. T. Suzuki (repr. London: Routledge & Kegan Paul Ltd., 1968) (first publ. 1952), p. 57; AK, III. 195–96. On his use of superpowers to help others see the Jātakas, tr. H. T. Francis and H. A. Neil, *Birth Stories of the Buddha* III–IV (London: Cambridge University Press, 1897); III, pp. 190–91, 230, 270; IV, pp. 10, 71ff., 207, 215, 231, 233–34, etc.

No. 47 AK, loc. cit. On the three classes of enlightened persons—Arhat, Pratyekabuddha, and Buddha—see Conze, *Buddhist Thought,* op. cit., pp. 166ff. On their ranking see, e.g., *Milinda's Questions,* tr. I. B. Horner, Sacred Books of the Buddhists, Vol. 22 (London: Luzac & Co., 1964), I, p. 147; *The Questions of King Milinda,* tr. T. W. Rhys-Davids, SBE Vols. 35–36 (London: 1890; repr. Delhi: Motilal Banarsidass, 1965), I, p. 158.

No. 48 For Candrakīrti's example (the bandits infesting a town), see Th. Stcherbatsky, *The Conception of Buddhist Nirvāṇa* (repr. Varanasi: Bharatiya Vidya Prakashan, undated), p. 284. For a survey of descriptions of the indefinable state, see Conze, *Buddhist Thought,* op. cit., pp. 69–79.

No. 49 Verses by Saraha, tr. Snellgrove, op. cit., v. 60–61. Mkhas, op. cit., Ch. 9. On the four initiations and four bodies, Mkhas, p. 324; Wayman's translation, however, lacks sufficient attention to the tense of the verbs; one should read "Now, the way in which the seeds of the four bodies were cast by the four initiations, and how they (the bodies) will be obtained, is very important." See also Beyer, op. cit., p. 401; Guenther, *Mystification,* p. 140, and refs., n. 3. For the flower initiation see Mkhas, pp. 291, 315. The flask is pictured by Beyer, p. 409; the twenty-five substances listed, ibid., p. 290.

No. 50 Mkhas, op. cit., pp. 316–21.

No. 51 Verse from Buddhaghosa, *Visuddhimagga,* ed. Henry Clark Warren, Harvard Oriental Series Vol. 41 (Cambridge, Mass.: Harvard University Press, 1950), p. 436; cf. Lamotte, *Histoire,* p. 45. Description from *Avadāna-śataka,* cited Conze, *Buddhism,* op. cit., p. 94.

No. 52 Descriptive paragraph adapted from Walpola Rahula, tr., *Le Compendium de Super-Doctrine (Philosophie Abhidharmasamuccaya) D'Asaṅga,* tr. Walpola Rahula (Paris: Publications de l'École Francaise d'Extrême-Orient, 1971), pp. 104–5. Verse of Bhavya cited in the *Lam-sgron* of Atīśa, tr. R. F. Sherburne, *Historical and Textual Background of the Enlightenment Path and its Commentary* (University of Washington, 1972), unpubl. M.A. thesis, p. 123. Cf. Gampopa, op. cit., pp. 232–33; Dalai Lama XIV, op. cit., p. 83. This square is the center of the board.

No. 53 Verses Sherburne, op. cit., pp. 113, 115. The roots of liberation from Asaṅga *Abhisamayālaṁkāra* (abbrev. *Abhisamaya.*), tr. Edward Conze, SOR. Vol. 6 (Rome: ISMEO, 1954), pp. 64–65. On the four right efforts (literally *prahāṇa,* "rejections"), see Har Dayal, op. cit., pp. 101ff. Cf. Gampopa, op. cit., pp. 232–33; Dalai Lama XIV, op. cit., p. 88.

No. 54 On this concentration see MHV, No. 532. Cf. Conze, *The Large Sutra on Perfect Wisdom* I, Oriental Studies Foundation (London: Luzac & Co. Ltd., 1961), p. 143, and Lamotte, *Traité,* Vol. III (Publications de l'Institute Orientaliste de Louvain, 1970), pp. 1,124–25 (on the four bases of psychic power); Gampopa, op. cit., pp. 232–22; Dalai Lama XIV, op. cit., p. 83.

No. 55 Verse after Sherburne, op. cit., pp. 76, 108. Paragraph *Abhisamaya.,* op. cit., p. 65. Wayman, op. cit., pp. 213–14, identifies "heat" and "climax" as dealing with the emptiness of self, "receptivity" and "highest dharmas" with the emptiness of phenomena. This is a neat division but not in accord with *Abhisamaya.,* pp. 77–80. See also MSA, XIV, p. 24 and n.; AK, VI. 163; Gampopa, op. cit., p. 229; Rahula, op, cit., p. 106; F. Edgerton, *Buddhist Hybrid Sanskrit Dictionary,* (repr. Delhi: Motilal Banarsidass, 1970), p. 281b.

No. 56 Verse after Sherburne, op. cit., pp. 77, 109. See also *Abhisamaya.,* op. cit., pp. 65, 77–80; MSA, XIV. 26; Rahula, op. cit., p. 106; Gampopa, op. cit., p. 233; Dalai Lama XIV, op. cit., p. 84.

No. 57 Verses from *The Royal Song of Saraha,* tr. H. V. Guenther (Seattle: University of Washington Press, 1969), p. 70. See ibid., pp. 9–10n., on *saha-ja.* Mkhas, op. cit., pp. 320–25; Guenther, *Mystification,* op. cit., p. 146. On the chakras and nerve system see Govinda, op. cit., pp. 140ff. This text was written in a monastery for the initiation of monks; for the initiation of female yogis (yoginis) no similar text has been translated.

No. 58 Mkhas, op. cit., p. 324; cf. the translation of Wayman, ibid., p. 325. Compare the four stages of the Kagyu Mahāmudrā, Milarepa, op. cit., pp. 98–99. On "rank of the Buddha" (sampuṭa), see Mkhas, pp. 156n., 266–69n.

No. 59 Hoffman, op. cit., pp. 123–30; TPS, pp. 212, 221, 598–99, and Pl. 211–13; Wylie, *Geography of Tibet,* p. 123, n. 72; Bacot, op. cit., p. 92n. Trungpa, *Visual Dharma,* Pl. 18. Picture of an actual Kālacakra mandala Wayman, op. cit., p. 80. JA, 1914, p. 146; TP, 1913, p. 596. In *Visual Dharma* the name of the Shambhala dynasty is misspelled *rig-ldan* for *rigs-ldan,* with the consequent misinterpretation. The Sanskrit name is Kulika, "good family."

No. 60 TPS, pp. 552–53, Pl. 153–54; Tāranātha, op. cit., pp. 208–9, 281–82; Samuel Beal, *Si-yu-ki: Buddhist Records of the Western World* (London: Trubner & Co., 1884), II, p. 233; see also Tāranātha, op. cit., pp. 191–92, on the journey of Śāntivarman via an old route underground. Translations done at Shambhala are noted in the catalogues; see G. Tucci, "The Sea and Land Travels of a Buddhist Sādhu in the Sixteenth Century," *Indian Historical Quarterly* 1931, pp. 693–94.

No. 61 Verse from *Guhyasamāja Tantra,* ed. Benytosh Bhattacharya, Gaekwad's Oriental Series No. 53 (Baroda: Oriental Institute, 1967), Ch. VII, v. 1; cf. the translation of Snellgrove in *Buddhist Texts,* p. 222. On this tantra and Urgyan see TPS, pp. 212–14; on Urgyan-pa's journey, ibid., pp. 158–59; BA, p. 701. See also Wylie, *Geography of Tibet,* p. 114, n. 2; IHQ, op. cit., 688–89. On the life of Padmasambhava see TPS, pp. 373ff.

No. 62 BA, pp. 839–40. For a classical Hindu account of the various Indian schools see Madhava Ācārya, *Sarva-darśana-saṁgraha,* tr. E. B. Cowell and A. E. Gough, repr. Chowkhamba Sanskrit Series Studies, Vol. X (Varanasi: Vidya Vilas Press, 1961); cf. W. T. de Bary et al., *Sources of Indian Tradition* (repr. Delhi: Motilal Banarsidass, 1958), Chs. I and III.

No. 63 AK, VI. 165; Rahula, op. cit., p. 106; MSA, p. 167; verse of Nāgārjuna from Gampopa, op. cit., p. 216.

No. 64 This stage is called, literally, "highest worldly dharmas" because one realizes the highest doctrines but still on a worldly level; they have not yet been put into practice. Rahula, op. cit., p. 107; MSA, p. 167; *Abhisamaya.,* pp. 66, 80; Wayman, op. cit., p. 213.

No. 65 *The Nine Ways of Bön,* tr. Snellgrove, pp. 193–95, 221–23, 229, 237.

No. 66 Verse adapted from Milarepa, op. cit., p. 618, cf. p. 623, n. 2. On initiation in general see Beyer, op. cit., pp. 423ff. The paths correlated with death and rebirth, ibid., pp. 119ff.; Wayman, op. cit., pp. 210ff.; Mkhas, op. cit., pp. 312–13n., 331–33; TPS, pp. 247–48. On the bodhisattva stages of the sutra vehicle, with which the tantric are correlated, see Dayal, op. cit., pp. 283–91 (the *Daśabhūmika Sūtra*), 278–91 (the *Bodhisattva-bhūmi*).

No. 67 A. L. Basham, *The Wonder That Was India* (New York: Grove Press, 1954), pp. 317–18; *Encyclopaedia of Religion and Ethics,* ed. James Hastings (New York: 1917–27), II, p. 810a; VII, p. 321b; *Mahāvastu,* op. cit., I, p. 237 (on siddha-devas); *Tāranātha,* op. cit., pp. 151–52 (on vidyādharas and the origins of tantra); cf. ibid., pp. 166, 187, 201, 253, 278–80; S. C. Das, *A Tibetan-English Dictionary* (repr. Delhi: Motilal Banarsidass, 1970), p. 1,179b (names of vidyādharas and their city). On the vidyādhara-piṭaka see TPS, p. 220, *Tohoku Catalogue,* No. 3,317; Lalmani Joshi, *Studies in the Buddhistic Culture of India* (Delhi: Motilal Banarsidass, 1967), pp. 210, 341, n. 96; Edgerton, op. cit., p. 488. Vaiśravana is sometimes said to be lord of vidyādharas, TPS, p. 573; they are termed attendants of Shiva by the Hindus, Sir Monier Monier-Williams, *A Sanskrit-English Dictionary* (London: Oxford University Press, 1899), p. 964a. For the summary of a story involving the vidyāharas from Indian literature, see A. K. Warder, *Indian Kāvya Literature,* Vol. II (Delhi: Motilal Banarsidass, 1974), para. 677ff.

No. 68 Das, *Dict.,* p. 181a. For the name Pure (Land) of the Astronauts, "space coursers" (dag-pa mkha'-spyod) see the *Book of the Dead* text (Varanasi: E. Kalsang, Buddhist Temple, 1969), p. 39; tr. Evans-Wentz, op. cit., p. 126; tr. Fremantle-Trungpa, op. cit., p. 54. Both the translations take *spyod* as "realm," as though for *spyod-yul.* This is incorrect. The heavenly realms are never *spyod-yul,* which indicates "sensory range," but always *zhing-khams,* "Buddha field" or "pure land." *Spyod* by itself, as in this name, means "coursing" or "enjoyment" (the latter being *longs-spyod*). *Mkha'-spyod* is the translation of the Sanskrit *khecara,* "space courser," the poetic term for a bird, and here applied to the "Pure Abode" (*dag-pa*) of those whose primary characteristic is the ability to fly (cf. Mkhas, op. cit., p. 220n.). This term is one step higher than dakini, *mkha'-gro-ma,* "female skygoer." Likewise Avalokiteśvara is known as *mkha'-spyod-pa,"* "astronaut," "sky courser," because he flies about the universe helping others. On the attainment of long life see Mkhas, op. cit., p. 201.

No. 69 Quote from BA, p. 812, on the translator Bsod-nams rgya-mtsho (A.D. 1424–82); on his turning the wheel see ibid., pp. 827ff. Cf. Milarepa, op. cit., p. 399; Mkhas, op. cit., pp. 315–17 (referring these traits to the tenth-stage bodhisattva); Beyer, op cit., p. 253.

No. 70 *Book of the Dead,* text, pp. 28–29; Fremantle-Trungpa, pp. 21–22, 47–48; Evans-Wentz, pp. 115–16; Getty, op. cit., p. 42. On the *shang-shang* garuda see Das, *Dict.,* op. cit., p. 1,230a. On the five Buddha families see Govinda, op. cit., p. 108ff.; Tucci, *Indo-Tibetica,* op. cit., III, 1, pp. 78–90, 145–59. On this form of Tārā see David Snellgrove, *The Hevajra Tantra* (London: Oxford University Press, 1959), I, pp. 137–38.

No. 71 *Daśabhūmika-sūtra,* tr. Megumu Honda, Sata-piṭaka Series V. 74 (New Delhi), pp. 127–43; MSA, p. *21; *Abhisamaya.,* pp. 22–53, 68–70, 80–85; Gampopa, op. cit., pp. 240–42; Dayal, op. cit., pp. 130ff.;

Śāntideva, *Śikṣā.*, pp. 265–69. For meditations on the identity of self and others see Śāntideva, BCA, VIII, v. 90 to end. On the ten perfections and the ten stages see also Candrakīrti, *Madhyamakāvatāra,* tr. L. de la Vallée Poussin, Le Muséon, 7–8, 11–12 (1907–11 ed. contains the first six chapters only).

No. 72 The lists of eight siddhis differ. Cf. Beyer, op. cit., pp. 246–47, 252–53; Mkhas, op. cit., pp. 220–21n. We have followed that of Geshe, op. cit., p. 311. For the way of siddhi vs. the way of study (*grub bka'-'dzin, bshad bka'-'dzin*), see BA, p. 962; TPS, p. 90. For some reservations by Atīśa regarding the former way, see Sherburne, op. cit., v. 60–61; for a refutation of objections see BA, p. 107. Among "ordinary" siddhis these are of the middling variety. For the lesser, see Rudra (No. 16); for the greater, see Desire, Form Wisdom-holders, and the Tantric Wheel-Turning King (Nos. 67–69). See also Wayman, op. cit., pp. 114–15 for the tokens of siddhi—sword, etc. On the classes of accomplishment, see Beyer, op. cit., pp. 246ff. For a list of "eight doctrines of siddhi" (*sgrub-pa bka'-brgyad*) see Beyer, pp. 43–45 and refs., 479–80, n. 82; Trungpa, *Visual Dharma,* Pl. 50.

Nos. 73–75 No. 66, op. cit. Verse in No. 74 from Saraha, tr. Snellgrove, op. cit., p. 232, v. 60.

No. 76 Fremantle-Trungpa, op. cit., pp. xviii–xix, 18–19, 44–45; Getty, op. cit., p. 37; Wayman, op. cit., p. 34.

No. 77 TPS, Pl. 23, H, comm. pp. 348–51; Pl. 39, comm. pp. 364–65; Pl. 49–50, comm. pp. 370–71; Fremantle-Trungpa, op. cit., pp. xix, 19–20, 46–47; Mkhas, op. cit., p. 34; Wayman, op. cit., p. 34. The classical description of Sukhāvatī is contained in *Sukhāvatī-vyūha sūtras,* tr. F. Max Muller, SBE Vol. 49 (London: Oxford University Press, 1894). See also Richard Robinson, *The Buddhist Religion,* The Religious Life of Man Series (Belmont, Calif.: Dickenson Publishing Co., 1970), pp. 66–69.

No. 78 *Daśabhūmika.*, pp. 166–73; MSA, pp. xx–xxi, 15–16, 34; *Abhisamaya.*, p. 24; Gampopa, op. cit., pp. 244–45. On the thirty-seven "factors of enlightenment" see Dayal, op. cit., Ch. IV.

No. 79 *Daśa.*, pp. 155–65; MSA, pp. *21–22, xx–xxi, 33b; Gampopa, op. cit., pp. 243–44; *Abhisamaya.*, p. 23 (for the five preparations for this stage).

No. 80 *Daśa.*, pp. 144–54; MSA, pp. *21, xx–xxi, 33a; Gampopa, op. cit., pp. 242–43; *Abhisamaya.*, p. 23 (for the eight preparations for this stage).

No. 81 For paths of maturation (first five stages) and liberation (last five) see Mkhas, op. cit., p. 331. Other references as for No. 66.

No. 82 Mkhas, op. cit., pp. 198n., 327; Guenther, *Mystification,* pp. 141–42, 146. Verse by Saraha, tr. Snellgrove, op. cit., p. 230, v. 48.

No. 83 Mkhas, op. cit., pp. 265, 327; Guenther, *Mystification,* pp. 72–73, 142–46; Beyer, op. cit., p. 136. Verses from Milarepa, op. cit., pp. 128–29.

No. 84 Mkhas, op. cit., pp. 21–27, 35, 39, 205n., 215; Hsüan Tsang, *Siddhi,* pp. 440–41, 696. The literal title of this square is "lesser Akaniṣṭha," indicating that it represents the highest realm of this Mount Meru world system, rather than the Ghanavyūha, "dense array," Akaniṣṭha which is the highest heaven of the world system called the "Adornment with flowery floors in inner chambers." This latter world system consists of $1,000^3$ (one thousand cubed) numbers of Meru systems, and is the abode of Vairocana, Vajradhara, or Samantabhadra Buddha (depending on which sect is making the description). Mkhas, op. cit., p. 205; Bu-ston, op. cit., I, pp. 131–32. On the karma producing the gods of this heaven, a "mixed state of trance," see AK, VI. 213.

No. 85 *Vimalakīrti,* op. cit., pp. 363–66; TPS, Pl. 2, comm. p. 332; Pl. 14–22, comm. pp. 347–48; Fremantle-Trungpa, op. cit., pp. xiii, 17–18; Getty, op. cit., pp. 5, 36–37; Wayman, op. cit., p. 331; Robinson, op. cit., p. 66.

No. 86 *Daśa.,* pp. 199–213; MSA, pp. *22, xx–xxi, 37a; Gampopa, op. cit., pp. 247–48. On the twenty attachments to be rejected and twenty positive attributes of this stage see *Abhisamaya.,* pp. 25–26.

No. 87 *Daśa.,* pp. 185–98; MSA, pp. *22, xx–xxi, 14, 36; Gampopa, op. cit., pp. 246–47; *Abhisamaya.,* pp. 24–25.

No. 88 *Daśa.,* pp. 174–84; MSA, pp. *22, xx–xxi, 15–16, 35; Gampopa, op. cit., pp. 245–46; *Abhisamaya.,* p. 24 (on the ten requisites for this stage). Regarding the name "hard to conquer," Candrakīrti makes the more obvious interpretation, that it is all but impossible for māras and other hindrances to obstruct him in his meditations (Dayal, op. cit., p. 288).

No. 89 Mkhas, op. cit., p. 327; Guenther, *Mystification,* p. 146; Beyer, op. cit., pp. 136–37. Verse by Milarepa, op. cit., p. 489.

No. 90 Mkhas, loc. cit. Passage quoted from the biography of Bu-ston, translated Beyer, op. cit., pp. 134–35; cf. the translation of David Ruegg, *The Life of Bu Ston Rin Po Che,* SOR, (Rome: ISMEO, 1966), pp. 82ff.

No. 91 Mkhas, op. cit., pp. 264n., 326–27. Verses by Saraha tr. Snellgrove, op. cit., pp. 238–39, v. 107–10.

No. 92 Conze, *Thought,* pp. 233–34; Gampopa, op. cit., pp. 265–66; Bu-ston, *History,* I, p. 131; *Abhisamaya.,* pp. 98–102 (the major and minor marks). The three bodies of the Buddha are depicted together in Evans-Wentz, *Liberation,* p. 192.

No. 93 Conze, *Thought,* pp. 232–33; Gampopa, op. cit., pp. 251–52, Ch. 20; *Abhisamaya.,* pp. 96–98 (its qualities and functions). Nāgārjuna's *Para-mārtha-stava,* Tibetan ed., tr. (in French) L. de la Vallée Poussin, Le Muséon, XIV (1913), pp. 16–18.

No. 94 *Daśa.,* pp. 256–76; MSA, pp. *23, xx–xxi, 14, 16, 38b; Gampopa, op. cit., pp. 250–51.

No. 95 *Daśa.,* pp. 273–75; MSA, pp. xx–xxi, 38a; Gampopa, op. cit., pp. 249–50; *Abhisamaya.,* pp. 27–28 (on the twelve dharmas of this stage).

No. 96 *Daśa.,* pp. 214–36; MSA, pp. *22–23, xx–xxi, 37b; Gampopa, op. cit., pp. 248–49; on the ten powers of the Buddha, ibid., p. 33ff. *Abhisamaya.,* p. 27 for the eight deeds of the bodhisattva on this stage.

No. 97 Tibetan *sku-bsdams-pa.* On the Emanation body see *Abhisamaya.,* p. 102; Gampopa, op. cit., pp. 266–67. Śākya-muni was born in about 566 B.C. and lived some eighty years—Lamotte, *Histoire,* pp. 13–25. Other sources on his life: André Bareau, *Recherches sur la biographie du Bud-dha* (Paris: Publications de l'École Française d'Extrême Orient, Vol. 53, etc., 1963, 1970); W. W. Rockhill, *The Life of the Buddha and the Early History of His Order, Derived from Tibetan Sources* (London: Kegan Paul, French, Trubner & Co., 1907); E. G. Thomas, *The Life of the Buddha* (London: Kegan Paul, French, Trubner & Co., 1931); Bu-ston, op. cit., I, p. 133ff.; II, pp. 7–72; A. Coomaraswamy, *Buddha and the Gospel of Buddhism,* 1916 (repr. New York: Harper & Brothers); A. Foucher, *La Vie du Bouddha, d'après les Textes et les Monuments de l'Inde* (Paris: Payot, 1949).

Nos. 98–99 Ibid.

No. 100 See esp. Bareau, op. cit., II, pp. 156–71. On Māra see also T. O. Ling, *Buddhism and the Mythology of Evil* (London: Allen & Unwin, 1962); *Vimalakīrti,* pp. 204–6n. At ibid., pp. 204–11, the great layman receives the daughers of Māra, refusing to let them return, and makes of them bodhisattvas. At pp. 259–61 he describes the bodhisattva as a "false Māra" who tempts beings with pleasures to bring them to the thought of enlightenment.

No. 101 Verses from Coomaraswamy, op. cit., pp. 35–36.

No. 102 *Dharmacakra-pravartana.* Bu-ston, op. cit., II, pp. 41–56. These ac-tivities—the Awakening and the first teachings—take place at night be-cause this is May–June, the hot season in India.

No. 103 *Prātihārya.* Bareau, op. cit., Ch. VI; Rockhill, op. cit., pp. 79–82; Thomas, op. cit., p. 91.

No. 104 *Nirvāṇa* is translated into Tibetan as "transcendence of suffering" (*mya-ngan las 'das-pa*). References as for No. 97. The directions read: *sprul-sku kun-la khyab-pa.*

·°⚬ Glossary ⚬°·

Terms are given in English or Sanskrit unless otherwise indicated. The correct Sanskrit transliteration is used even if it has been modified in the text. "Tt." indicates the Tibetan transliteration, according to the system of T. V. Wylie, University of Washington. One cannot guess at Tibetan pronunciation from its spelling: Consult your local lama!

ARHAT (Tt. *dgra-bcom-pa*) Ideal of the "Lesser Vehicle." One who has become Awakened but without having made the resolve to help other beings attain that state. More generally, the term for any Awakened personage.

ASURAS (Tt. *lha-ma-yin*) "Antigods." Jealous deities often at war with the devas (gods) of the lower heavens (see square No. 15).

ATĪŚA Indian teacher who came to Tibet in 1042 and aided the reformation and spread of Buddhism.

ATTAINMENT See SIDDHI.

AVALOKITEŚVARA (Tt. *spyan-ras-gzigs*) A bodhisattva great hero, the "lord who looks down" with compassion; special patron deity of Tibet.

AWAKENING (*bodhi,* Tt. *byang-chub*) Also, ENLIGHTENMENT. The conquest of karmic necessity and understanding of the true nature of the world; elimination of the bonds to continued birth and death.

BARDO (Tibetan term; Sanskrit: *antarābhava*) The "intermediate" state between death and one's next rebirth, in which consciousness takes a "mind-made body" formed by karmic tendencies.

216

BODHI See AWAKENING.

BODHICITTA (Tt. *byang-chub sems*) "Thought of enlightenment": the intention of the bodhisattva to win nirvana for himself and others. In tantric yoga, the union of wisdom and means as symbolized by semen and menstrual blood.

BODHISATTVA (Tt. *byan-chub sems-dpa'*) The hero or ideal of the Greater Vehicle. An "enlightenment being" whose resolve is to attain nirvana and to bring all living beings to that state. Any practitioner of the Greater Vehicle. More strictly, one who has attained the first of ten bodhisattva stages.

BODHISATTVA GREAT HERO (bodhisattva-mahāsattva) A tenth-stage bodhisattva on the threshold of Buddhahood.

BODHISATTVA VOW The formalized resolve of a bodhisattva, made in a ritual context at the beginning of one's career in the Greater Vehicle.

BODHI TREE The Sāl tree at the present Bodhgaya under which the Buddha was enlightened.

BRAHMĀ (Tt. *tshangs-pa*) Chief of the god of the lower levels of the Realm of Form. The god conceived as creator of the world and father of living beings.

BRAHMANA Hindu religious caste. Especially a priest of the god Brahmā.

BUDDHA FIELD See PURE LAND.

ḌĀKINĪ (Tt. *mkha'-'gro-ma*) "Skygoer." Tantric female adept or teacher with powers to change form, fly through the sky, etc.

DELUSION OF SELFHOOD (*ātma-vāda*) Illusion that there exists a permanent and abiding principle in living beings and phenomena.

DEVA (Tt. *lha*) A god inhabiting one of the six heavens of the Realm of Sense Desire.

DHARMA (Tt. *chos*) All forms of the doctrine of the Buddha and its elaboration by Buddhists. RELIGION in general. Also, DHARMAS (in lower case): The elements of reality, PHENOMENA.

DHARMA BODY (*dharma-kāya,* Tt. *chos-sku*) The pure, unoriginated, and all-pervading form of the Buddha as the absolute principle of Awakening (see square No. 93). Also, the corpus of Buddha's doctrines.

DHARMA-DHĀTU (Tt. *chos-dbyings*) "Element of Dharma." The essential nature of Dharma and of dharmas; emptiness, the absolute principle of things. The realm of the Dharma.

DHYĀNA (Tt. *bsam-gtan*) Meditation in general. The four stages of meditative trance.

EMANATION BODY (*nirmāṇa-kāya,* Tt. *sprul-sku*)   The physical form of the Buddha as it appears to ordinary beings (see square No. 97).

ENJOYMENT BODY (*sambhoga-kāya,* Tt. *longs-spyod sku*)   The large and marvelous physical form of the Buddha as manifest to tenth-stage bodhisattvas (see square No. 92).

ENLIGHTENMENT   See AWAKENING.

GOD   The gods, including devas, of the three Realms: Sense Desire, Form, and Formless Realm. In particular Brahmā, a god of the Realm of Form and considered by some to be creator of the world.

GREATER VEHICLE (*mahāyāna,* Tt. *theg-pa chen-po*)   Buddhist doctrine and practice based on the emptiness of all phenomena and aimed at the attainment of Buddhahood and the liberation of all living beings.

HIGH AWARENESS (*abhijñā,* Tt. *mngon-shes*)   The six supernormal faculties of sense, gained through meditation (see square Nos. 39 and 94).

HUNGRY GHOSTS   See PRETAS.

INDEPENDENT BUDDHA (*pratyeka-buddha,* Tt. *rang sangs-rgyas*)   The yogi who attains Awakening without the aid of a Buddha or his teachings in his last lifetime.

INDRA (Tt. *dbang-po*)   Chief of the gods of the Heaven of the Thirty-three.

KUMBHĀṆḌAS (Tt. *grul-bum*)   Monstrous demigods somewhat like vampires in Western mythology.

LESSER VEHICLE (*hīnayāna,* Tt. *theg-pa dman-pa*)   See VEHICLE OF THE DISCIPLES.

MĀDHYAMIKA (Tt. *dbu-ma-pa*) SCHOOL   The "middle way" of the Mahāyāna, teaching ultimate relativity of all phenomena.

MAHĀYĀNA (Tt. *theg-pa chen-pa*)   See GREATER VEHICLE.

MAṆḌĀLA (Tt. *dkyil-'khor*)   The circle of a Buddha or of some aspect of the enlightenment principle. The circle of bodhisattvas and disciples surrounding a Buddha in his pure land. Also, the circular diagram of the pure land of a Buddha or other deity for purposes of initiation of tantric visualization.

MANTRA (Tt. *gsang-sngags*)   Set of Sanskrit syllables activating the energy or qualities of a particular deity or power.

MĀRA (Tt. *bdud*)   King of the devas of the highest heaven in the Realm of Sense Desire (see square No. 32), so lord of this whole realm. Any demon or obstacle to meditation—a fear or desire that arises as distraction (see square No. 100).

MIND-ONLY or THOUGHT-ONLY (Tt. *sems-tsam*) SCHOOL The idealistic school of the Mahāyāna, teaching that all phenomena are products of consciousness.

NĀGAS (Tt. *klu*) Great serpents inhabiting springs and bodies of water. They have human torsos and heads and can be fierce or benign. They hoard great treasures (see square No. 13).

NIRVĀṆA (Tt. *mya-ngan las 'das*) Transcendence of suffering. Synonym: liberation. Antonym: sàmsāra.

PĀLI CANON An ancient set of Buddhist texts redacted in this dialect of Sanskrit and preserved in Śrī Laṅka and Southeast Asia, belonging to one of the schools of The Vehicle of the Disciples. See also THERAVĀDA.

PANDIT One who is learned, especially in Sanskrit.

PARINIRVANA The Buddha's final entry into nirvana, as opposed to the nirvana that continues to function in the world.

PRATYEKABUDDHA See INDEPENDENT BUDDHA.

PRETAS (Tt. *yi-dwags*) Ghosts and demonic spirits. Especially hungry ghosts (see square No. 10).

PURE LAND (*kṣetra*, Tt. *zhing-khams*) The realm created by the magic power of a Buddha in which living beings can be born, enjoy the essentials of life and beauteous surroundings, and listen to the Dharma without obstruction. Also, BUDDHA FIELD.

SĀDHANA (Tt. *sgrub-thabs*) Tantric ritual meditation aimed at the re-formation of reality through visualization, gesture, and mantra.

ŚĀKYAMUNI (Tt. *śākya thub-pa*) The sage of the Śākya tribe. The historical Buddha whose teachings, in the sixth and fifth centuries B.C., established the Buddhist doctrine in our age.

SAMSĀRA (Tt. *'khor-ba*) The cycle of death and rebirth. The six karmic destinies.

SIDDHI (Tt. *dngos-grub*) The attainment that comes from successful accomplishment of a tantric ritual meditation.

WORLDLY SIDDHI or ATTAINMENT Magical powers of a lower, middling, or higher order for altering reality that come of such meditation (see square Nos. 67–69, 72).

SUPREME SIDDHI   The attainment of Buddhahood by means of ritual identification.

SIDDHA (Tt. *grub-thob*)   A tantric adept.

STUPA (Tt. *mch'od-r-ten*) ·Sacred place to house relics.

SUBJECT/OBJECT DUALITY (grāhya-grāhaka)   Illusion of a separate existence of perceiver and perceived, self and other.

SUPERKNOWLEDGES   See HIGH AWARENESS.

SUTRA (Tt. *mdo*)   Scripture as spoken by the Buddha of the Greater or Lesser vehicle, as distinguished from TREATISE and TANTRA.

TANTRA (Tt. *rgyud*)   The class of Buddhist scripture that teaches the Vajrayāna. More generally, a branch of Mahāyāna practice involving radical and intensive meditative techniques to the attainment of Buddhahood.

TĀRĀ (Tt. *sgrol-ma*)   Female bodhisattva of the tenth stage and goddess of compassion: "savioress."

THERAVĀDA (*Sthaviravāda*)   The view of the Elders, referring to the senior disciples of the Buddha, who were the monastic leaders of the early community. One of the schools of the Vehicle of the Disciples. The Buddhism of Śrī Laṅka and parts of Southeast Asia.

THOUGHT OF ENLIGHTENMENT or AWAKENING   See BODHICITTA.

THREE JEWELS (*triratna*, Tt. *dkon-mchog-gsum*)   The three sources of refuge: the Buddha, his Dharma, and the Buddhist community.

TRANCE   See DHYĀNA.

TREATISE (*śāstra*, Tt. *bstan-bcos*)   Writings by Buddhist scholars on Dharma and related subjects, in accord with SUTRA.

VAJRA (Tt. *rdo-rje*)   The hardest possible substance, ADAMANTINE   A tantric ritual object, symbolizing indestructibility, the bodhisattva's skill in means as opposed to his wisdom, the male principle. In tantric yoga, the male organ.

VAJRA HELL   The special hell reserved for malpracticeers of the tantra, those who break their vows (see square No. 1).

VAJRA BODY   The indestructible body of the Buddha, his relics enshrined in a stupa that have survived cremation.

TOTAL VAJRA (*viśva-vajra*, Tt. *kun-nas rdo-rje*)   A symbol of indestructibility with four vajras facing in all directions. See picture on the game board of square No. 1—Vajra Hell.

VAJRA-PĀṆI (Tt. *phyag-na rdo-rje*)   A tantric bodhisattva in fierce form holding a vajra, thunderbolt, as weapon. Converter of fierce energies to the service of the Dharma.

VAJRAYĀNA The vajra vehicle, a synonym for Buddhist tantra.

VEDAS The ancient scriptures of Hinduism, some dating as early as 10,000 B.C.

VEDIC GODS The thirty-three devas of Indian antiquity.

VEHICLE OF THE DISCIPLES (*Śrāyaka-yāna,* Tt. *nyan-thos theg-pa*) The doctrine and practices of certain close disciples of the Buddha that aim at arhatship and one's own liberation from sàmsāra.

VIDYĀ (Tt. *rig-pa, rig-sngags*) Knowledge—either worldly science or spiritual wisdom. In tantric symbolism, the female principle equal to wisdom (prajñā): woman, concrete or imagined, playing the role of wisdom being united with the male, Skill in Means.

VIDYĀDHARA (Tt. *rig-'dzin*) One who has mastered knowledge or wisdom, especially tantric attainment; a class of wise and powerful beings. More generally, an accomplished master of tantra.

WISH-GRANTING JEWEL (Tt. *yid-bzhin nor-bu*) Magical jewel that grants one's every wish, the possession of a Wheel-turning King.

YĀKṢAS (Tt. *gnod-sbyin*) Demigods inhabiting trees and mountains; these demigods are objects of popular cults and can be beneficent or harmful.

YOGIN (Tt. *rnal-'byor-pa*) One who practices yoga. Any meditator, whether Buddhist or not, but especially a practitioner of the tantras. Female form: YOGINI (Tt. *rnal-'byor-ma*).

·⚬❦ Appendix ❧⚬·

The Alternative Ways to Reach Each Square

Square No. 1

Move here from: Tantra, Lesser Path of Accumulation (No. 33).

Square No. 2

Move here from: Hot Hells (No. 3), or Barbarism (No. 21).

Square No. 3

Move here from: Interminable Hell (No. 2), Howling Hells (No. 4), Rope and Crushing Hells (No. 5), Demons (No. 14), Hinduism (No. 22).

Square No. 4

Move here from: Rope and Crushing Hells (No. 5), Reviving Hell (No. 6), Hungry Ghost (No. 10), Asura (No. 15), Bön (No. 23), Formless Realm (No. 36).

Square No. 5

Move here from: Hot Hells (No. 3), Howling Hells (No. 4), Cold Hells (No. 7), Temporary Hells (No. 8), Animals (No. 11), Demons (No. 14), Disciples, Accumulation (No. 38).

Square No. 6

Move here from: Howling Hells (No. 4), Cold Hells (No. 7), Temporary Hells (No. 8), Jambu Island (No. 17), Divine Highway (No. 24), Four Great Kings (No. 27), Independent Buddhas, Accumulation (No. 43).

222

Square No. 7

Move here from: Hot Hells (No. 3), Rope and Crushing Hells (No. 5), Temporary Hell (No. 8), Thirty-three (No. 28), Mahāyāna, Lesser Accumulation (No. 52).

Square No. 8

Move here from: Hot Hells (No. 3), Howling Hells (No. 4), Reviving Hell (No. 6), Hungry Ghost (No. 10), Mahāyāna, Middle Accumulation (No. 53), Bön Wisdom-holder (No. 65).

Square No. 9

Move here from: Vajra Hell (No. 1).

Square No. 10

Move here from: Interminable Hell (No. 2), Hot Hells (No. 3), Howling Hells (No. 4), Rope and Crushing Hells (No. 5), Reviving Hell (No. 6), Cold Hells (No. 7), Animals (No. 11), Divine Animals (No. 12), Nāga (No. 13), Asura (No. 15), Western Continent (No. 18), Barbarism (No. 21), Hinduism (No. 22), Heavenly Highway (No. 24), Four Great Kings (No. 27), No Fighting (No. 29), Ruling Others' Emanations (No. 32).

Square No. 11

Move here from: Hot Hells (No. 3), Rope and Crushing Hells (No. 5), Cold Hells (No. 7), Temporary Hell (No. 8), Hungry Ghost (No. 10), Divine Animals (No. 12), Nāga (No. 13), Asura (No. 15), Western Continent (No. 18), Eastern Continent (No. 19), Barbarism (No. 21), Heavenly Highway (No. 24), Thirty-three (No. 28), Formless Realm (No. 36), Disciples, Accumulation (No. 38), Mahāyāna, Lesser Accumulation (No. 52).

Square No. 12

Move here from: Reviving Hell (No. 6), Animals (No. 11), No Fighting (No. 29), Emanation Gods (No. 31), Pure Abodes (No. 37).

Square No. 13

Move here from: Rope and Crushing Hells (No. 5), Animals (No. 11), Hungry Ghost (No. 10), Western Continent (No. 18), Eastern Continent (No. 19), Hinduism (No. 22), Wheel-turning King (No. 26).

Square No. 14

Move here from: Howling Hells (No. 4), Temporary Hell (No. 8), Hungry Ghost (No. 10), Asura (No. 15), Bön (No. 23).

Square No. 15

Move here from: Cold Hells (No. 7), Divine Animals (No. 12), Nāgas (No. 13), Demons (No. 14), Eastern Continent (No. 19), Northern Continent (No. 20), Barbarism (No. 21), Hinduism (No. 22), Heavenly Highway (No. 24), Mahāyāna, Middle Accumulation (No. 53), Bön Wisdom-holder (No. 65).

Square No. 16

Move here from: Tantra, Lesser Accumulation (No. 33).

Square No. 17

Move here from: Interminable Hell (No. 2), Reviving Hell (No. 6), Animals (No. 11), Demon (No. 14), Northern Continent (No. 20), Heavenly Highway (No. 24), Wheel-turning King (No. 26), Four Great Kings (No. 27), Thirty-three (No. 28), No Fighting (No. 29), Realm of Form (No. 35), Formless Realm (No. 36). ·

Square No. 18

Move here from: Cold Hells (No. 7), Four Great Kings (No. 27), Ruling Others' Emanations (No. 32).

Square No. 19

Move here from: Temporary Hells (No. 8), Hungry Ghost (No. 10), Northern Continent (No. 20), Disciples, Application (No. 39).

Square No. 20

Move here from: Wheel-turning King (No. 26), Thirty-three (No. 28), Independent Buddhas, Application (No. 44).

Square No. 21

Move here from: Nāga (No. 13), Divine Animals (No. 12), Asura (No. 15), Western Continent (No. 18).

Square No. 22

Move here from: Jambu Island (No. 17), Thirty-three (No. 28), Delight in Emanations (No. 31).

Square No. 23

Move here from: Four Great Kings (No. 27), Noncontention (No. 29).

Square No. 24

Start of the game only.

Square No. 25

Move here from: Demon (No. 14), Jambu Island (No. 17).

Square No. 26

Move here from: Jambu Island (No. 17).

Square No. 27

Move here from: Animals (No. 11), Divine Animals (No. 12), Nāga (No. 13), Western Continent (No. 18), Northern Continent (No. 20), Bön (No. 23), Heavenly Highway (No. 24), Realm of Form (No. 35), Independent Buddhas, Application (No. 44).

Square No. 28

Move here from: Divine Animals (No. 12), Nāga (No. 13), Asura (No. 15), Northern Continent (No. 20), Wheel-turning King (No. 26), Four Great Kings (No. 27), Ruling Others' Emanations (No. 32), Disciples, Application (No. 39), Disciples, Vision Cultivation (No. 40), Independent Buddhas, Vision (No. 45).

Square No. 29

Move here from: Bön (No. 23), Wheel-turning King (No. 26), Thirty-three (No. 28), Independent Buddhas, Cultivation (No. 46).

Square No. 30

Move here from: No Fighting (No. 29), Delighting in Emanations (No. 31), Ruling Others' Emanations (No. 32), Realm of Form (No. 35), Disciples, Vision Cultivation (No. 40), Independent Buddhas, Application (No. 44), Independent Buddhas, Cultivation (No. 46), Independent Buddhas, Arhatship (No. 47), Mahāyāna, Lesser Accumulation (No. 52).

Square No. 31

Move here from: No Fighting (No. 29), Disciples, Vision Cultivation (No. 40).

Square No. 32

More here from: Delight in Emanations (No. 31), Disciples, Vision Cultivation (No. 40).

Square No. 33

Move here from: Beginning Tantra (No. 25), Tantra, Middle Accumulation (No. 41), Wisdom-holder of the Eight Siddhis (No. 72).

Square No. 34

Move here from: Yama (No. 9), Rudra (No. 16), Action-Completion (No. 70).

Square No. 35

Move here from: Ruling Others' Emanations (No. 31), Disciples, Vision Cultivation (No. 40), Independent Buddhas, Cultivation (No. 46).

Square No. 36

Move here from: Realm of Form (No. 35).

Square No. 37

Move here from: Realm of Form (No. 35), Disciples, Accumulation (No. 38), Independent Buddhas, Cultivation (No. 46), Independent Buddhas, Arhatship (No. 47), Disciples, Arhatship (No. 51), Mahāyāna, Middle Accumulation (No. 53).

Square No. 38

Move here from: Jambu Island (No. 17), Western Continent (No. 18), Eastern Continent (No. 19), Beginning Tantra (No. 25), Formless Realm (No. 36), Independent Buddhas, Accumulation (No. 43), Mahāyāna, Lesser Accumulation (No. 52), Hindu Wisdom-holder (No. 62).

Square No. 39

Move here from: Disciples, Accumulation (No. 38), Independent Buddhas, Application (No. 44).

Square No. 40

Move here from: Disciples, Accumulation (No. 38), Disciples, Application (No. 39), Independent Buddhas, Vision (No. 45), Mahāyāna, Middle Accumulation (No. 53).

Square No. 41

Move here from: Tantra, Lesser Accumulation (No. 33), Desire Wisdom-holder (No. 67), Form Wisdom-holder (No. 68), Wisdom-holder of the Eight Siddhis (No. 72).

Square No. 42

Move here from: Demon (No. 14), Tantra, Lesser Accumulation (No. 33), Tantra, Middle Accumulation (No. 41), Shambhala (No. 59), Mahāyāna, Receptivity (No. 63), Desire Wisdom-holder (No. 67), Form Wisdom-holder (No. 68).

Square No. 43

Move here from: Eastern Continent (No. 19), Delight in Emanations (No. 31), Disciples, Application (No. 39), Independent Buddhas, Application (No. 44), Independent Buddhas, Vision (No. 45), Bön, Wisdom-holder (No. 65).

Square No. 44

Move here from: Independent Buddha, Accumulation (No. 43).

Square No. 45

Move here from: Independent Buddha, Application (No. 44).

Square No. 46

Move here from: Independent Buddha, Application (No. 44), Independent Buddha, Vision (No. 45).

Square No. 47

Move here from: Independent Buddha, Vision (No. 45), Independent Buddha, Cultivation (No. 46).

Square No. 48

Move here from: Independent Buddha, Arhatship (No. 47), Disciples, Arhatship (No. 51).

Square No. 49

Move here from: Tantra, Greater Accumulation (No. 42), Shambhala (No. 59), Mahāyāna, Highest Teachings (No. 64), Form Wisdom-holder (No. 68).

Square No. 50

Move here from: Tantra, Greater Accumulation (No. 42), Tantra, Application: "Heat" (No. 49), Shambhala (No. 59).

Square No. 51

Move here from: Independent Buddha, Cultivation (No. 46).

Square No. 52

Move here from: Jambu Island (No. 17), Hinduism (No. 22), Bön (No. 23), Joyful Heaven (No. 30), Delighting in Emanations (No. 31), Realm of Form (No. 35), Pure Abodes (No. 37), Disciples, Accumulation (No. 38), Disciples, Application (No. 39), Independent Buddhas, Accumulation (No. 43), Independent Buddhas, Vision (No. 45), Independent Buddhas, Arhatship (No. 51), Hindu Wisdom-holder (No. 62), Bön Wisdom-holder (No. 65).

Square No. 53

Move here from: Joyful Heaven (No. 30), Mahāyāna, Lesser Accumulation (No. 52).

Square No. 54

Move here from: Joyful Heaven (No. 30), Pure Abodes (No. 37), Mahāyāna, Lesser Accumulation (No. 52), Mahāyāna, Middle Accumulation (No. 53).

Square No. 55

Move here from: Joyful Heaven (No. 30), Mahāyāna, Middle Accumulation (No. 53), Mahāyāna, Greater Accumulation (No. 54), Shambhala (No. 59).

Square No. 56

Move here from: Mahāyāna, "Heat" (No. 55).

Square No. 57

Move here from: Mahāyāna, "Heat" (No. 55), Tantra, "Climax" (No. 50).

Square No. 58

Move here from: Tantra, "Receptivity" (No. 57).

Square No. 59

Move here from: Tantra, Middle Accumulation (No. 41), Tantra, Greater Accumulation (No. 42), Mahāyāna, Greater Accumulation (No. 54), Form Wisdom-holder (No. 68).

Square No. 60

Move here from: Tantra, Middle Accumulation (No. 41), Mahāyāna, Greater Accumulation (No. 54), Shambhala (No. 59).

Square No. 61

Move here from: Mahākāla (No. 34).

Square No. 62

Move here from: Barbarism (No. 21), Hinduism (No. 22).

Square No. 63

Move here from: Joyful Heaven (No. 30), Mahāyāna, Greater Accumulation (No. 54), Mahāyāna, "Heat" (No. 55), Mahāyāna, "Climax" (No. 56), Shambhala (No. 59), Potāla (No. 60).

Square No. 64

Move here from: Joyful Heaven (No. 30), Pure Abodes (No. 37), Mahāyāna, "Climax" (No. 56), Potāla (No. 60), Mahāyāna, "Receptivity" (No. 63).

228

Square No. 65

Move here from: Bön (No. 23).

Square No. 66

Move here from: Tantra, "Climax" (No. 50), Tantra, "Receptivity" (No. 57), Tantra, "Highest Teachings" (No. 58).

Square No. 67

Move here from: Tantra, Middle Accumulation (No. 41), Wisdom-holder of the Eight Siddhis (No. 72).

Square No. 68

Move here from: Wisdom-holder Among the Desire Gods (No. 67).

Square No. 69

Move here from: Wisdom-holder Among the Desire Gods (No. 67), Second Tantra (No. 73).

Square No. 70

Move here from: Mahākāla (No. 34).

Square No. 71

Move here from: Mahāyāna, "Highest Teachings" (No. 64), Action-Completion (No. 70), Land of Bliss (No. 77), Super-joy (No. 85).

Square No. 72

Move here from: Beginning Tantra (No. 25).

Square No. 73

Move here from: Tantra, "Receptivity" (No. 57), Tantra, "Highest Teachings" (No. 58), First Tantra (No. 66), Action-Completion (No. 70), Jeweled Peaks (No. 76), Super-joy (No. 77).

Square No. 74

Move here from: Tantra, "Highest Teachings" (No. 58), First Tantra (No. 66), First Sutra (No. 71), Jeweled Peaks (No. 76), Land of Bliss (No. 77).

Square No. 75

Move here from: First Tantra (No. 66), Tantric Wheel-turning King (No. 69), Second Tantra (No. 73), Third Tantra (No. 74).

Square No. 76

Move here from: Superjoy (No. 85).

Square No. 77

Move here from: Tantra, "Receptivity" (No. 57), Mahāyāna, "Receptivity" (No. 63), Mahāyāna, "Highest Teachings" (No. 64).

Square No. 78

Move here from: Jeweled Peaks (No. 76), Second Sutra (No. 80), Third Sutra (No. 79).

Square No. 79

Move here from: First Sutra (No. 71), Second Sutra (No. 80).

Square No. 80

Move here from: First Sutra (No. 71).

Square No. 81

Move here from: Mahākāla (No. 34), Tantric Wheel-turning King (No. 69), Second Tantra (No. 73), Third Tantra (No. 74), Fourth Tantra (No. 75).

Square No. 82

Move here from: Fourth Tantra (No. 75).

Square No. 83

Move here from: Urgyan (No. 61), Fourth Tantra (No. 75), Fifth Tantra (No. 81), Sixth Tantra (No. 82).

Square No. 84

Move here from: Urgyan (No. 61), Seventh Tantra (No. 83), Eighth Tantra (No. 89), Ninth Tantra (No. 90), Tenth Tantra (No. 91), Tenth Sutra (No. 94), Ninth Sutra (No. 95).

Square No. 85

Move here from: Tantra, "Highest Teachings" (No. 58), Mahāyāna, "Receptivity" (No. 63).

Square No. 86

Move here from: Sixth Sutra (No. 87).

Square No. 87

Move here from: Fourth Sutra (No. 78), Fifth Sutra (No. 88).

Square No. 88

Move here from: Fourth Sutra (No. 78), Third Sutra (No. 79).

Square No. 89

Move here from: Fifth Tantra (No. 81), Sixth Tantra (No. 82).

Square No. 90

Move here from: Sixth Tantra (No. 82), Eighth Tantra (No. 89).

Square No. 91

Move here from: Seventh Tantra (No. 83), Ninth Tantra (No. 90).

Square No. 92

Move here from: Fourth Tantra (No. 75).

Square No. 93

Move here from: Supreme Heaven (No. 84), Tenth Tantra (No. 91), Tenth Sutra (No. 94).

Square No. 94

Move here from: Ninth Sutra (No. 95), Eighth Sutra (No. 96).

Square No. 95

Move here from: Seventh Sutra (No. 86), Fifth Sutra (No. 88), Eighth Sutra (No. 96).

Square No. 96

Move here from: Seventh Sutra (No. 86), Sixth Sutra (No. 87).

Square No. 97

Move here from: Enjoyment Body (No. 92).

Square No. 98

Move here from: Adopting a Physical Form (No. 97).

Square No. 99

Move here from: Setting Forth (No. 98).

Square No. 100

Move here from: Ascetic Practices (No. 99).

Square No. 101

Move here from: Conquest of Māra (No. 100).

Square No. 102

Move here from: Buddhahood (No. 101).

Square No. 103

Move here from: Turning the Wheel of Dharma (No. 102).

Square No. 104

Move here from: Demonstration of Miracles (No. 103).